Mohamed Sifaoui is an Algerian journalist based in Paris. He writes for *Marianne* and *La Voix du Luxembourg*, and has made documentaries on Islamism for the television channel France 2.

INSIDE AL QAEDA

HOW I INFILTRATED THE WORLD'S DEADLIEST TERRORIST ORGANIZATION

MOHAMED SIFAOUI

Translated from the French by George Miller

THUNDER'S MOUTH PRESS
NEW YORK

Inside Al Qaeda

Copyright © 2003 by Le Cherche Midi Editeur

Published by
Thunder's Mouth Press
An Imprint of Avalon Publishing Group Incorporated
245 West 17th Street, 11th Floor
New York, NY 10011

First published in the U.S. by Thunder's Mouth Press 2004

First published in France as *Mes "Frères" Assassins*
by Le Cherche Midi 2003

First published in the U.K. by Granta Books 2003

Library of Congress Cataloging-in-Publication Data is available.

ISBN: 1-56025-610-9

9 8 7 6 5 4 3 2 1

Printed in the United States of America
Distributed by Publishers Group West

To all the victims of Islamist terrorism

*To my Algerian colleagues who were victims of
Islamist killers' bullets*

*To Allaoua Aït Mebarek, Mohamed Dorbhane, and
Djamel Derraza, my colleagues from* Soir d'Algérie, *killed in
February 1996 by an Islamist bomb*

*To my friend Richard, who lost his daughter in
a terrorist attack in Paris on 25 July 1995*

FOREWORD

I am an Algerian Muslim by birth, and a journalist by profession. Like everyone else in Algeria, I had lived with the scourge of Islamist terrorism for a decade before the western world discovered the horror of 11 September 2001. Like many of my fellow Algerians, I have lost many people close to me, both family and friends. Such traumas have left indelible marks which will never heal.

In Algeria we have lived through this turmoil without the sympathy of the international community. To put it bluntly, the West didn't really care about terrorism until it came knocking at its own door. I have never experienced the solidarity shown by the Europeans towards the Americans, for example, in the aftermath of the attacks on Washington and New York. On 11 September, I understood something very important: no matter what anyone says, and despite the views that continually get repeated, in the West, the life of an Algerian isn't valued as highly as the life of an American, and a Rwandan life isn't worth as much as a European one.

Nonetheless, realizing this has not stopped me carrying on my fight against Islamism, since I do not want to see it strike France and threaten the security of the country which has welcomed me and which has become mine. I have never given up the fight, even though there are certain sectors of public opinion here in France which continue to look the other way, and make a distinction between 'moderate' Islamism and 'radical' fundamentalism, often excusing *en passant* the crimes committed in the name of this form of fascism all around the world, not least in Algeria. Along with thousands of others worldwide I have continued to denounce Islamism as the ideology which feeds a despicable form of terrorism, and which threatens whole societies from the Philippines to Chechnya, and from the Near East to the Horn of Africa. All the while, bomb attacks continue with terrible regularity.

For those who may not be able to imagine the feelings of trauma and devastation which a bomb attack causes, I shall describe the one that I personally escaped.

It was a quiet February afternoon in 1996. Algiers was bathed in spring sunlight. I was in the newspaper office where I worked as a journalist along with some of my colleagues. The atmosphere was calm. We were in the middle of the month of Ramadan. I was hurrying to finish my article so that I could leave the office and take a walk round the market. One of my colleagues, Hocine, came to get me out of the office because he had a joke he wanted to tell me. It was that joke which saved my life, because we had only just stepped outside when we felt a huge explosion. In a fraction of a second, the

2

newspaper offices were razed to the ground. I had left my colleagues behind in the office, and I found them there, as still as if they were asleep, beneath piles of rubble, girders and dust. But they weren't asleep: Mohamed Dorbhane, a talented journalist and father of four, had been killed instantly; Djamel Derraza, a father of two and our crossword-setter, had been torn to pieces; Allaoua Aït Mebarek, our editorial director, a confirmed bachelor and an artist who loved life, lay dead too. Outside, around thirty passers-by whose only fault was to have been in the wrong place at the wrong time had also lost their lives. A van packed with 300kg of TNT had blown up several buildings. The sky over Algiers had darkened, and it was in the name of Islamism that it darkened.

That day I realized something fundamental: I absolutely had to fight against the fascist ideology of the Islamists and those who supported it, so that I would never again have to leave somewhere simply hoping that a bomb wouldn't go off.

In the investigation published here, I have faced up to my responsibilities. If I have taken risks and in doing so exposed my family to certain danger and an uncertain future, it is definitely not through any pursuit of celebrity on my part, nor is it out of courage or heroism. It is above all through conviction, a conviction which is strengthened every time I read in some sections of the press the horrific attempts to excuse fundamentalism or justify terrorism, and every time I hear the 'human rights' justification which goes almost as far as blaming the victim and sympathizing with the perpetrators. A similar sort of behaviour allowed Hitler to come to power in the first place, then to cause war, and finally to exterminate millions of Jews on account of the fact that they were Jews.

I refuse to allow Islamism and its supporters to terrorize our children and endanger the future of our society. That is why the moment I had the chance to infiltrate an Islamist network, I took it, in order to reveal how its structures work, structures which are designed solely to stir up hatred and cause terror in civil society.

The account which follows is the diary I kept for three months in which I recorded everything I saw, heard and observed in the course of my contact with the Islamists, the people whom I came to call 'my brothers'. My hope is that this story will contribute to a greater understanding of both Islamism, and its counterpart, terrorism.

INTRODUCTION

On 1 October 2002, in Paris, the high court trial opened of the two men accused of the attacks which struck the French capital in 1995. The accused, Boualem Bensaïd and Smaïn Aït Ali Belkacem, are Islamists who belong to the GIA (the Armed Islamist Group). This is a terrorist organization which for ten years has been relentlessly committing the worst atrocities in Algeria against the general public, intellectuals, journalists and the security forces, with the aim of bringing about the collapse of the Algerian state and replacing it with theocratic rule.

It was with this end in mind that the organization – which had succeeded in extending its network into several Western and Arab countries and setting up sleeper cells in some European countries, particularly France, Great Britain, Germany, Belgium and Switzerland – decided some time in late 1994 or early 1995 to export its 'holy war' to France to try to provoke the French government into withdrawing its support for 'the apostate regime in Algiers'. In fact, since 1993 and the arrival of Edouard

Balladur as Prime ·Minister, the hornet's nest of Islamism in France had been stirred up. This new awareness of the threat it posed replaced the complacency of governments of the left, who had not welcomed the suspension of the electoral process in Algeria. This had been declared by the army, and was supported by large sections of society because it blocked the way to the Islamists of the FIS (Islamic Salvation Front) and thereby avoided the country turning into another Afghanistan.

The court[1] therefore had to reach a judgement on two terrorists who had been sent to France by Djamel Zitouni, then the infamous head of the GIA, to orchestrate and execute a wave of attacks which were to cost the lives of eight people and injure more than two hundred others. This lengthy trial, which went on until 31 October 2002, inevitably attracted the interest of a public who were especially worried about security in the aftermath of 11 September.

For my part, I intended to follow the trial from start to finish. I had several reasons for doing so: first there were professional ones – I had been asked to cover it by the editor of *La Voix du Luxembourg*, the Luxembourg paper I write for. In addition, as I had published a book[2] the previous month on Islamism and the terrorist threat, I continued to take a keen interest in any event linked to Islamist terrorism. I had an interest dating back as far as

---

1. The defendants were tried without jury before a special court of seven full-time magistrates used for terrorist trials.
2. *La France malade de l'islamisme: Menaces terroristes sur l'Hexagone* (le cherche midi, 2002)

1995, when the attacks took place, and it was all the keener on account of a certain element in France which stubbornly tries to excuse Islamist terrorists and argues without any evidence that their terrible acts are the work of the Algerian secret service. This trial would therefore allow the truth to come out. And so there were plenty of reasons why I did not want to miss a single moment of it. It was a decision I would not regret . . .

To understand what happened later, I must briefly go back to the attacks of 1995 and the trial itself. On 11 July 1995, the imam of the mosque on the rue Myrrha in Paris's 18th *arrondissement* was murdered along with one of his assistants. Two weeks later a bomb exploded on an RER underground train at the Saint-Michel station. Between July and September 1995, several more attacks were carried out. Yet other bomb attacks fortunately failed, often because of a fault in the explosive device's detonation mechanism. After an investigation that lasted several weeks, the police identified a first terrorist cell active in the Lyons region, which was run by Khaled Kelkal, a young delinquent who had found his way into Islamism. The cell consisted of several members who were either close to Algerian terrorist groups or at the very least sympathized with international Islamist terror. Previously there had been another cell in Chasse-sur-Rhône which had been taken apart. This was made up of Islamists of Algerian origin and young converts to Islamism, and gave the terrorists logistical support.

Kelkal had been identified thanks to fingerprints found on a gas cylinder which was intended to explode on the Lyons–Paris TGV line. After a hunt which lasted several days, the terrorist from Lyons was shot by the police near the Malval woods in the city. Before that, another Islamist, Karim Koussa, had been wounded; a few days before Kelkal was killed, Koussa had exchanged shots with the police to cover the escape of his accomplice and childhood friend. It was the clues found after the Lyons cell was put out of action and in the course of numerous interrogations which would make possible the arrest of other members of the group. That was how Nassreddine Slimani, whose identity papers had been used to cover the activities of certain members of the group, came to be taken in for questioning by the police. It was claimed that he was going to head up a new cell in Lyons. Boualem Bensaïd, who met Nassreddine Slimani in Paris and gave him instructions for bomb making, was arrested in Paris in early November 1995. Bensaïd, the 'emir' of the GIA, came from Algeria specially to coordinate the wave of attacks with Smaïn Aït Ali Belkacem, who had been very active in the Lille region and was making preparations to carry out attacks there.

So this whole terrorist web had to be reconstructed during the trial, and what interested me greatly as a journalist was that there still remained grey areas in the case: first of all, the main protagonists were absent from the list of the accused. Ali Touchent, long considered the 'brains' of the operation, had been eliminated in Algiers in May 1997, after returning to Algeria from France via a third country, allegedly using false papers. Khaled Kelkal, head of the Lyons cell, was dead, and Rachid Ramda who, according to information in the file, had financed terrorist operations from London, was being detained there, and the British authorities were refusing to extradite him to France.

I couldn't believe that the wave of attacks had been carried out by only four fundamentalists; the dock seemed too large for just the two accused. I remained convinced that they had had other accomplices who were still at large. It was with the intention and in the hope of finding out more that I decided to undertake an investigation. But where to start? The case was certainly complicated enough for the security forces, so how could I find out more? At that moment, I would never have believed that a few weeks later I would find myself at the heart of an Islamist cell in Paris.

In the course of my work as a journalist, especially when I was travelling in Afghanistan and Pakistan, I have often passed myself off as an Islamist. I find this easy since I am a Muslim, and can say without conceit that I know the Islamists' ideology inside out. Unfortunately, I also have a significant handicap: as I have frequently expressed my opinion on questions relating to Islamism and terrorism in books, articles and on television, I'm not unknown to the Islamists. Nonetheless, I decided to try my luck.

The story which follows is therefore an account of my experiences during my three months with Islamists whose aim was to take part in the armed struggle. These Islamists already carry out clandestine activities as logistical support to the terrorists who engage in actual operations. They are known to the security forces and certainly monitored by them, but continue despite this to serve the cause of jihad in various ways, as I shall explain.

KARIM AND MY NEW 'BROTHERS'

On the first day of the trial I noticed a few fundamentalists in court who had evidently come to support their 'brothers'. One of them attended so diligently that he aroused the curiosity of a good number of observers.

One of these Islamists spoke to the media on the first day; his speech, like his outward appearance, left no doubt as to his ideological allegiances – he was a committed fundamentalist who wholeheartedly supported the two accused. He told journalists that his name was Mehdi Terranova. Son of a Lebanese mother and a father of Sicilian origin, this young man, who was built like a giant, was obviously a convert to Islam.

I took advantage of his readiness to talk and asked him some questions. I especially wanted to find out if he knew Boualem Bensaïd and Smaïn Aït Ali Belkacem. He said he did. How did he know them? He had 'played sport' with Bensaïd and was 'a cousin' of Aït Ali Belkacem. These claims sounded like lies to me: a young Frenchman with a Sicilian father and a Lebanese mother, who had an Algerian cousin would be rather unusual.

In reality, as I discovered a few weeks later, Mehdi had got to know them in prison. He had been arrested for a criminal offence in 1995 and converted to Islam after meeting the Islamist prisoners. Mehdi's real name was Rudy Terranova and he was the stepson of a gangland boss, Jean-Pierre Paul, who was murdered in Paris in 1995 in a score-settling killing. His mother committed suicide a few weeks later, and after a fight Mehdi left one of the men who was behind the murder of his stepfather for dead. That was how he came to be in prison when he was only sixteen. He was freed when he turned eighteen and joined the French army. There he trained with crack troops and took courses in explosives and firearms, before leaving the army to devote himself to the Islamist cause.

Mehdi and two other bearded men followed the trial that first day standing at the back of the courtroom. This worried and exasperated the prosecution, who took their presence as a provocation, especially as they were continually exchanging winks and gestures with the two accused.

In *La Voix du Luxembourg* on Thursday 3 October 2002, I ended my article like this: 'three bearded men standing at the back of the court smile and exchange winks with the accused. These men introduce themselves to journalists as the cousins of the men on trial. Worrying . . .'

I could not have guessed that a few weeks later, I would be calling these men my 'brothers'.

Luck on My Side

By the end of the first week of the trial my beliefs about Islamism had been confirmed. The two accused had made a complete volte-face; after confessing everything to the police and the examining magistrates pre-trial, in court they denied it all outright, even when presented with evidence. Boualem Bensaïd pushed this to ridiculous extremes when he refused to recognize his own identity photograph on a fake administrative document. While the prosecution was shocked by such behaviour, the men standing at the back of the courtroom made plain with some show of irony and a fair amount of arrogance that the provocative attitude of the two accused delighted them.

I worked all through the weekend from Friday to Sunday, 4–6 October. I had planned to film a report for TV on Islamic terrorist networks in Europe, and so I had phoned some of my contacts in London and Madrid, whom I'd worked with before, to sort out the angle we wanted to take. I was also going through my documents looking for material relating to the investigation into the Paris attacks. And I was in talks with a TV station and a production company about a big documentary project, though nothing had been finalized. In any case, there was no question of beginning it that month and dropping my coverage of the trial.

*

Mehdi and the other two Islamists had followed the first week of the trial, but in the second week he was absent, as was one of the others. Only the third man – who was aged around thirty, and wore a beard and traditional Pakistani dress, and had long hair in a ponytail – turned up at the Palais de Justice almost every day to follow the trial. This man, whose behaviour intrigued me, was very discreet and never struck up a conversation with anyone. He stared at everyone during the recesses in the trial and returned to court as soon as proceedings resumed. I saw him, however, discussing something with Smaïn Aït Ali Belkacem's lawyer, maître Van der Meulen. I decided I would speak to him, though I was in no hurry; I told myself that I had to wait for the best possible moment to approach him. The glances he shot me from time to time made me think that he had recognized me, as my photo had appeared on the book I had published the month before.

I waited until Thursday 10 October, when, during a recess, I found myself by chance face to face with the bearded man. We made eye contact and disingenuously I ventured the following: 'Excuse me, you're a Muslim, aren't you?'

Surprised and perhaps taken aback by my question, he replied, 'Yes! Yes, I'm a Muslim.' He might well have added, 'Why? Isn't it obvious?'

To drive the point home, I added, '*Asslam-o-Alaikum* [Peace be with you], I'm a Muslim too.' I shook his hand.

He gave the impression that he was delighted that someone had spoken to him like this and he began to talk about the trial: 'You've seen how they treat Muslims, brother?'

I asked him if he knew the two accused. 'Yes, I know them,' he replied. I didn't want to show any sign of inquisitiveness, at least for the moment. I suggested, however, that we left the Palais de Justice and went for a coffee somewhere. He agreed. So we went towards the exit, heading for the nearby Place du Châtelet. On the way, my new 'friend' revealed that he recognized my face. I've had it, I thought to myself, my gamble hasn't paid off. During the previous two years I had been in the media many times – I'd had a public debate with an unscrupulous publisher and another with people who insisted on trying to clear the fundamentalists, especially the Algerians, of their crimes; I'd had two books published with my photo on the back cover; I'd made several appearances on different TV channels and written comment columns in the press; in short, everything militated against me going unnoticed. I'd been rumbled. But to my great surprise, that wasn't what the man with the beard meant.

'You didn't go to school at the *lycée* Emir-Abdelkader in Bab el-Oued, by any chance?'

The question struck me like a blow to the head. I had indeed gone there for my secondary education in the 1980s.

'Yes,' I replied in astonishment.

'Weren't you in the same class as so-and-so and so-and-so?' He reeled off the names of my old classmates, all from the Bab el-Oued district. I hadn't come from that district of Algiers, but had chosen that *lycée* because several of my friends went there. It turned out I had gone to the same school as the man I was talking to. What a stroke of luck! He remembered my face but couldn't recall my name.

'I'm Djamel Mostaghanemi,' I told him confidently, as if to refresh his memory, before asking him in turn for his name.

'Karim Bourti,' he replied. So at last I knew the name of my Islamist. I was sure that this was his true identity, since he produced a work permit and an identity card to show me what he looked like before he became an Islamist, that is before he had a beard and ponytail, and before he wore a *djellaba* or Pakistani or Afghan dress.

I had just adopted a new identity, and I would have to sustain it for as long as I could. I also took on a new personality, a new way of expressing myself, and began preaching a message which was alien to me. I wanted to make myself credible to my new 'friend', who didn't waste any time in asking me detailed questions about my religious beliefs. I portrayed myself as a committed Islamist, but one who hadn't yet completed his ideological training; I didn't want to overplay my hand. My childhood memories and the other things I'd said had gained Karim's confidence. It was a good opportunity for me to cement the friendship quickly. I began praising the actions of the Algerian Islamists and recalling the 'Golden Age' of the FIS in Algeria. And I made a point of praising in passing the actions of Osama Bin Laden. I didn't need to say more; I had patently won Karim's trust. For an hour and a half we chatted on over our coffee, in particular about Islam and Algeria. I was the one who interrupted the discussion around 6.30 p.m. by reminding my companion that it was time for the *Maghreb* (evening) prayer.

We each went our separate ways. On my way home on the metro I couldn't help but reflect on the discussion I had just had.

I had been able to gather a fair number of details about Bourti: his name, where he lived and, most of all, details of his activism, as he had told me during our conversation that he had been sentenced to three years in prison for associating with known terrorists. Karim had been arrested as part of the sweep just before the 1998 World Cup and had been accused of planning terrorist attacks during the competition. Like all Islamists, he had protested loudly at the injustice of this.

When I got home I made straight for my computer and files on the 1998 arrests, and there I did indeed find Karim Bourti's name. He had been found guilty of associating with terrorists. His case had been closely linked to that of Omar Saiki, who was considered to be the head of the network dismantled a few weeks before the start of the World Cup. I had been really lucky – I had chanced upon a big fish. Despite the risks, I decided there and then that I had to carry out an investigation into him.

Nonetheless, experience told me to proceed with the greatest caution. I would have to act quickly so as to collect the maximum amount of information, but without giving the appearance of rushing. Above all, I had to avoid arousing Karim's suspicions, and let things seem to fall into place naturally. I spent the weekend thinking through my strategy.

*

The second week of the trial was given over to hearing the witnesses' evidence. Investigators and experts came to the witness box one by one to go over the elements of the case, and the evidence began to build up against the accused in spite of their stubborn denials. Everyone was aware that the following week an important witness was going to be called – Nassreddine Slimani, a young man from Lyons who had been sentenced to eight years in prison for association with terrorists. Slimani was a friend of Kelkal's and had been part of a Lyons cell before it was completely taken apart in 1995. As he wasn't present when the witnesses were called, the journalists had been speculating endlessly about whether he would turn up the following Monday, 14 October. I decided to go and find him, along with a fellow journalist from the France 2 channel who was also following the trial, so she and I caught the TGV to Lyons on Friday 11 October at around 5.30 p.m., accompanied by a film crew.

When we arrived, we hired a car to get us to Vaulx-en-Velin, the district of the city where most of the members of the Lyons cell who were implicated to a greater or lesser degree in the 1995 attacks were born. We looked in vain on the Minitel directory for Slimani's telephone number. We did, however, find the numbers of others with the same surname. This was our only lead, but after many enquiries which turned out to be wild-goose chases we had still not found our witness. Disappointed, we decided to go to our hotel. We did have the beginning of another trail, though: someone we had mistaken for Nassreddine Slimani had confirmed that he was related to our man and had said that he would help us find him the following day. We decided just in case to call directory enquiries and ask for the number of *all* the Slimanis living in the area, but although we dialled several numbers, this approach proved futile. Discouraged, we decided we would start afresh the next day.

Saturday 12 October 2002

We were in Vaulx-en-Velin by 9 a.m. We had been told about a
bakery run by someone called Slimani, but he got rid of me
quickly and said he didn't know the person we were looking for.
In the end, it was my colleague who managed to reach Slimani
by phone, by making her way through the list directory enquiries
gave us. She succeeded in getting him to agree to a meeting in
a café in Vaulx-en-Velin at 11.30. Our man already knew that
some journalists were looking for him. He agreed to a meeting
without cameras or microphones.

At the agreed time, a young man of around thirty turned
up. Clean-shaven and dressed in jeans, pullover and a brown
jacket, he seemed very different from the stereotype of an Islamic
fundamentalist. He looked well presented and intelligent, and
had a permanent hint of a smile on his face; this former
member of Kelkal's network appeared to be just a regular guy.
There was nothing to give away the fact that he was completely
in the grip of Islamist ideology and had supported, directly or
indirectly, the terrorists who had carried out attacks in Paris and
elsewhere.

We were going to invite him to sit down, but the café terrace
was completely full, so I proposed we went somewhere quieter.
He pointed out a pizzeria just a stone's throw away, which looked
promising as it was lunchtime. We suggested having something to
eat together, but he refused. I guessed that Slimani was fasting.

(Muslims often fast throughout the month which precedes Ramadan.) We began the conversation without any preamble: would he go into the witness box next Monday?

'I don't know yet,' was all he replied at first. So we went back over the 1995 attacks. Slimani confirmed that he had indeed given his identity papers to another member of the Kelkal network, Abdelkader Maameri, but he was unaware of the real use they were intended for. Maameri had told him that his papers would 'provide help for brothers who are illegal immigrants'.

'I just wanted to help,' he told us.

I might well have felt sympathetic to this young man if he had not, the next moment, shown a side of himself which is typical of the Islamic fundamentalist.

'Do you condemn the 1995 attacks?' I asked. This question revealed the young man and his 'charm' for what they were: he was a fundamentalist who approved of the death of innocent victims. His reply was enlightening: 'No, I don't condemn them. Who am I to condemn them? Only God can pass judgement and condemn.'

From that moment, this man could no longer appear innocent as far as I was concerned; he was guilty, even if he hadn't made or planted the bombs himself. When he met Boualem Bensaïd in Paris on 31 October 1995, Slimani had picked up a recipe for making explosive devices. This, copied onto a scrap of paper, had been found in his possession when he was arrested. This piece of evidence, contained in the judicial inquiry, had never been denied by Slimani.

I decided to bring up subjects which I knew would provoke him. 'Why did you pick up those bomb-making instructions?' I asked out of the blue. Slimani, who up till this point had been confident and smiling, showed evident discomfort when I confronted him with this question.

'That's a question I'd rather not answer.'

'Why? You say you're innocent and did nothing wrong.'

'I don't want to reply because it could make difficulties for other people.'

'Who?'

Slimani remained silent. Was he supposed to pass the instructions on to other people, whom the investigation failed to identify? Was he himself supposed to make a bomb and rebuild the Lyons cell after Khaled Kelkal had been eliminated? It was hard to say.

After more than two hours with Slimani, we parted, having arranged a meeting with him for the following Monday at the Palais de Justice.

We were almost certain he would turn up because during our interview he had said clearly, 'It is possible that I will go to testify because I was called by the defence. I wouldn't go if I'd been called by the prosecution.' Solidarity among Islamists is unshakeable.

I gave him my telephone number and told him my name was Djamel Mostaghanemi, the same alias I had given to Karim Bourti two days previously. I would not regret it . . .

I was home by late Saturday afternoon, and immediately began writing up my article. I didn't want to waste any time while the information was still fresh in my mind. Slimani hadn't wanted us to take notes, so in the train back to Paris we transcribed into our notebooks the conversation we had just had with Kelkal's former disciple.

Monday 14 October 2002

The trial of the two GIA Islamic activists was due to resume at
2 p.m. The journalists and the prosecution were wondering
whether Slimani would respond to his summons. I had only just
got to the court when two fellow journalists told me that they had
passed Slimani in the corridor, and when the trial reopened, he
was indeed there to face the court.

My immediate reaction was that I didn't recognize the
person we had met at the weekend. The smiling expression and
the manner of the well-brought-up young man had given way to
the true nature of the fundamentalist. Arrogance had supplanted
humility. Intolerance had taken over from kindness. In short, the
Islamist had taken over from the man. His testimony was marked
by incidents from beginning to end: first he refused to swear the
oath, next he showed no compassion for the victims of the
attacks, and finally he displayed a level of hypocrisy which knew
no bounds.

Whereas in our presence he had refused to condemn the
attacks, in front of the judges he confined himself to saying he
'didn't agree with' these acts, far from a clear condemnation of
attacks which had cost the lives of eight people and wounded two
hundred others. Islamists often use dissimulation; one of their
slogans is 'War is a ruse.'

At the end of his testimony, I made straight for Slimani. I
asked to see him outside and he agreed. I left the court first,

abandoning him to the mercy of the TV cameras, which pursued him, though he hid his face in the hood of his jacket. On my way out of the court, I bumped into Karim, who told me that he wanted to talk to Slimani.

'Do you know him?'

'Yes,' he replied, but added nothing more. I took advantage of the movement of the crowd to slip away from Karim. And then I caught sight of Slimani at the end of a corridor in the Palais de Justice. I hurried after him, with the cameramen still chasing him. When I did eventually catch him up, I was able to assure him there were no more journalists in pursuit. He greeted me and we left the court building together. When we got outside, I asked him for his impressions of the trial. Just like the first time we had met, he showed nothing but contempt for justice.

As we walked, we made small talk. He told me that he would be away for a couple of months on what he claimed was a foreign holiday. A two-month holiday for someone who has just got out of prison after a six-year term is fairly unusual. Where was the money coming from? That question still nags me. Before we parted, I persuaded him to give an interview to my colleagues from France 2. He refused at first, but eventually gave in to my persistence, and a few minutes later he was answering the journalists' questions. At the end of the interview, I told Slimani that Karim Bourti was looking for him.

'Where is he?' he asked, showing surprise that I knew him.

'He's still in court.'

'Can you tell him that I'll be waiting in the Place du Châtelet?'

'Of course,' I said, convinced that little details such as this could work in my favour and help me infiltrate their network.

I couldn't help feeling pleased at the way events were unfolding. It was confirmation of my belief that the Islamists implicated in terrorism almost always know each other, even when they are separated by hundreds or thousands of miles. Indeed this is one of the characteristics of these networks which today pose a threat to the peace of every corner of the world.

How did Slimani and Bourti know each other? From prison? Or were they already in contact in 1995? If the latter were the case, that suggests that Karim Bourti belonged to the network in 1995. I speculate on this because to this day members of the network responsible for the attacks on Paris are still at large, and the police investigators have several times suspected the existence of another Parisian cell whose members have still not been identified. Moreover, Karim Bourti, who knows Boualem Bensaïd and Smaïn Aït Ali Belkacem, arrived in France in late 1994 or early 1995, about the same time as two other GIA terrorists sent to France by Djamel Zitouni.

Back in the court, when the trial had resumed after a short recess, I found Karim standing as usual at the back of the room. I urged him to come outside, watched in astonishment by the police, who didn't understand what I could be up to with a Muslim fundamentalist. Outside I told him as requested that Slimani was waiting for him. Karim thanked me with a 'God bless you, my brother', visibly touched by this sign of attention. My new friend knew that at the trial he was on hostile ground. Everyone looked at him with distrust. I was the only person who spoke to him; I was playing my role of the complete hypocrite convincingly. Karim turned to go and join Slimani, the man who was possibly his accomplice, while I went back to the court to follow the proceedings.

After a fairly eventful day, Karim didn't turn up in court the following one. I was worried. It was the first time since the start of the trial that none of the Islamists had been present to support their brothers. In what had become a ritual, at the opening of each session the two accused would glance at the back of the room and then smile at Karim and Mehdi. But today Bensaïd scanned the room before lowering his eyes, apparently disappointed not to see his brothers. But his absence was shortlived and the next day Karim was back. I noticed him before the session began, while I was talking to some other journalists. I left them to go and sit beside Karim. He was pleased to see me. That day we had a long and very interesting talk . . .

Karim didn't ask a lot of questions, which was all to the good. He preferred to talk about his own case. He told me that he had been 'wrongfully imprisoned' and that the police hadn't found anything against him except his support for the claims of the GSPC, the *Groupe salafiste pour la predication et le combat* (the Salafist Group for Preaching and Combat – the Algerian terrorist group then directed by Hassam Hattab which has pledged itself to Al Qaeda) and some videos of the Chechen war and other terrorist propaganda. I listened without asking too many questions so as not to arouse his suspicions with too blatant curiosity. Karim openly claimed membership of Hattab's group.

Hattab, who had belonged to the GIA until the end of 1997, broke with the other Islamists and has become in recent years the leader of the most significant armed group in Algeria since the structures of the GIA were crushed by the anti-subversive effort.

Karim acknowledged that he belonged to the GSPC; I was, consequently, in the presence of a terrorist. I felt a strange sensation at that moment, a sort of sickening feeling, and I believe that if he had looked me in the eye, he would have been in no doubt what I think of people like him. I suggested going for a coffee to interrupt our conversation. I wanted to collect my thoughts.

On our way to the coffee machine, I regained my composure. It was imperative that I didn't give anything away. From that day on, I became cold and calculating, showing no outward sign of emotion. I would play my role right to the end, however much it pained me morally. I would have to feign pleasure when I heard a report of the death toll from Algeria. Like him, I would have to worship Bin Laden, call him 'the sheikh', applaud the attacks of 11 September, and express the wish that similar attacks would happen in France. I would have to trample my principles underfoot, deny my own values, and preach the things I have always fought against . . .

Karim cut short my reflection by confirming that Bensaïd and Aït Ali Belkacem had been sent to France by Djamel Zitouni in 1995. 'They are good people,' he said, adding, 'they're serious, those two. They were in the Algerian resistance and swore *bayaat al maout* [allegiance to death] to their emir, Zitouni.' I was stunned: my new 'brother' was giving me information of the greatest importance.

I decided to let him continue in this vein by asking him about the differences of opinion which undermine the Algerian terrorist groups.

'Hassan Hattab,' he told me, 'is opposed to the decision by the GIA to condemn the whole of the Algerian populace.' He explained that the GSPC had reserved two options: the internationalization, terrorism by following the path of Bin Laden, and the continuation of attacks in Algeria so as to wage a war of attrition on the regime there. I told Karim that I had been in favour of such a course of action for several years now and that what Osama Bin Laden was doing deserved support. Taken in by my words, Karim decided to say more.

'Djamel, we must never forget our main enemies. The Algerian authorities, I mean,' he said, as if to sound me out on this point.

'I haven't forgotten,' I said, 'but at my level all I can do is fight them through the media.'

'You can help us in another way, if you want.'

'How?'

'If you have information on prominent Algerians, especially in the military or people like Dalil Boubakeur [the rector of the Paris mosque] or Soheïb Bencheikh [the mufti of Marseilles], don't hesitate to tell me.'

'Why?' I replied, still keeping up my naivety.

With a fixed grin which was telling in itself, Karim gave me a response which sent a chill down my spine: 'Why do you think? To get rid of them.'

I assured my 'brother' Karim that he could count on my

active collaboration, and then reminded him that we should be getting back to the trial of our brothers. On our way to the court-room, I decided to reverse the roles.

'I want to confide in *you*, Karim. You know, I have chil-dren . . .' I said to test his reaction.

He stopped abruptly, looked me in the eye, and said, 'Listen to me, Djamel, we are the soldiers of God. Even if they cut us into pieces, we don't rat on our brothers.'

We walked on, discussing the political situation in Algeria. When we got to the courtroom, we separated. He resumed his place at the back of the room, and nodded to the two accused and to me sitting among the public. This happened under the puzzled gaze of the police and of several other people who couldn't understand what a journalist and an Islamist who asso-ciated with terrorists could have to say to each other. I didn't want too many people to see us together in case someone revealed, consciously or otherwise, my real identity and beliefs.

We got into the habit of having a conversation before each sitting of the court and during recesses. We always touched on the same subjects: the two accused, Bin Laden, Algeria, religion, the jihad and so on. In the course of one of our discussions, Karim told me that he played a very particular role in Paris: he collected money and distributed it among all the Islamists held in French prisons. Each week he sent money orders to the prisoners. I saw these money orders with my own eyes, at least those that he sent to Boualem Bensaïd, Smaïn Aït Ali Belkacem and Adel Mechat, another Algerian imprisoned for a terrorist incident. I noticed that he had a considerable amount of correspondence with the prisoners. He explained to me that 'sensitive information' was passed to Islamist prisoners via non-political prisoners as they were watched less closely. In fact, Karim confided this in order to ask me to take part in the collections on behalf of the prisoners.

Karim and I were getting on better and better. I continued to play my role and he suspected nothing. Each new day of the trial brought additional proof against the two accused, who nonetheless persisted with their denials. Bensaïd was as arrogant as ever, and Aït Ali Belkacem was just as shifty and just as susceptible to the charisma of his co-defendant, who was obviously the leader. At the end of each session, I spent half an hour with Karim discussing the arguments we'd heard. He was often beside himself with anger, and kept using the same phrases – 'the enemies of God', to talk about the magistrates, the police or the prosecution lawyers, 'brothers' or 'the mujahidin' to mean the accused, and 'hypocrites' for the media.

As the days went by, Karim came to feel at ease with me. To maintain this atmosphere, I sometimes recalled memories of our youth, our school, the teachers, the head, and even football. Karim rarely talked about such things. His life centred on religious activism. 'I am a Muslim,' he was fond of saying, 'and so I submit to God's will.' He willingly returned again and again to the subjects which really interested me; in particular he liked to talk about jihad (holy war). He told me his dream was to die 'a martyr for Allah's cause'. His eyes would mist over with tears when he talked about the 'great deeds of the brothers under arms' in Algeria, Afghanistan, and Chechnya. Through him, I was able to see the disaster which is caused by religious fanaticism. Every day he would express opinions which shocked me, but which I was obliged to agree with. This was all the more difficult for me as I had to demonstrate my approval with a nod of the head or a smile.

One day I was with Karim when a man who had lost his daughter in the Saint-Michel bombing said hello to me. Karim asked me who the person who had greeted me was. I replied that he was the father of one of the victims of the Saint-Michel attack. 'That man lost his daughter,' I said, searching his eyes for any hint of emotion.

'Who gives a damn about his daughter?' he responded with terrible coldness. 'Anyway, she's not even worth a prayer because she's an infidel.'

I had to hold myself back from throttling him or thumping him in the face. I calmed down, but I admit that I still haven't managed to get over his response. How can a human being become so insensitive? Are those who react in this way human beings? There is no religion, no belief, no fanaticism which can justify such an attitude. I am all the more revolted as these people who are devoid of all humanity speak in the name of my religion, Islam.

On 30 October 2002, after a five-week trial, the special court was due to give its verdict. The defence had attempted some sort of salvage operation. The magistrates had to come to a decision based on their deepest convictions about the case. That day, in addition to Karim, Mehdi was back, as was Nour, a young woman in a veil whom Karim introduced to me. According to him, this 'sister' had been Boualem Bensaïd's companion before his arrest in November 1995.

To gain more of their confidence, I pretended to share the Islamists' worries and showed concern for the two accused. I promised them that I'd carry out an investigative report to demonstrate the innocence of their fellow Muslims. In reality, I was taking the first steps for quite a different operation. When in the past I have done investigative reporting to show the danger posed by the Islamists, there have been people who have considered that what I revealed about the fundamentalists was 'exaggerated', or 'out of proportion'. I had sometimes regretted not being able to film them and record what they said and did. I had consequently promised myself that for *this* undercover operation, I would do something for TV, since what could be stronger than a picture to convince those who do not want to acknowledge the evidence? Isn't a picture worth a thousand words?

The verdict was expected in the course of the evening. I made the most of the time until then by having a long discussion with the Islamists. Even though I had revealed to Karim that I was a practising Muslim, I hadn't yet had the opportunity to pray with him. But that day I got my chance. I had noticed on previous days that Karim went off to pray by himself in a corner of the Palais de Justice. It was thus quite natural that I should suggest to my 'brother' that we went and fulfilled this fundamental requirement of Islam. This gesture counted in my favour as they were able to note that my behaviour squared with what I had told them. It is important to realize that Islamists are very particular about the time of prayers. They observe the timetable, following a ritual of their own as they are able to pray anywhere at all, with their shoes on, preferably in a group, and so on. I did exactly what they did, mimicking all their gestures, paraphrasing their words, and reciting perfectly all their invocations. My 'brothers' were reassured, as was clear from their attitude to me at the end of the prayer in which Karim took the role of imam.

Afterwards we talked at length about religion and dogma, and mentioned the Salafist theologians who inspire most of today's Islamist movements: Ibn Thaymia, inevitably, the hard-line imam of the twelfth century whose writings are today a work of reference; Mohamed Ibn Abdelwaheb, the nineteenth-century theologian who is behind the Wahabi ideology which is disseminated from the Arab peninsula, but also others such as the Egyptian, Sayed Qutb, and his predecessor, Hassan Al-Benna, who founded the 'Muslim brothers' at the beginning of the twentieth century in Egypt. We also talked about texts by other Wahabi scholars, such as the sheikhs Ibn Al-Baz and Otheimine who are considered the contemporary ideologues of Islamism. My knowledge of religion impressed them. They had never come across a journalist, they later told me, who was sympathetic to Islamist ideas. All the same, they pointed out that I should take Karim's course to complete my religious education.

At around 10 p.m. the judges announced their verdict: life for both the accused, and, in the case of Boualem Bensaïd, a minimum term of twenty-two years. Karim and Mehdi were thrown into a state. Mehdi left the court in a fury, shouting at the cameras: 'I swear in the name of Allah that they will not serve half that sentence. You will see what the wrath of Allah is like.' This extreme outburst was replayed that evening and the next day on most TV channels.

Outside the Palais de Justice, Smaïn Aït Ali Belkacem's lawyer came up to Karim to tell him that he was intending to appeal. 'Watch Canal Plus next Monday. There'll be new facts,' the lawyer said. But Karim didn't understand what he meant and he turned to me, looking for an explanation. I provided it: a team from the subscription channel had made a pseudo-investigation intended to get the Islamist killers off the hook and lay the 1995 attacks at the door of the Algerian authorities, at the same time suggesting that the French secret services were indirectly implicated. I looked at Karim as I explained that a report on TV would 'prove the innocence of our brothers'.

After such a long day, I decided to leave my new 'friends', but before I did, I arranged a meeting with Karim and told him we should stay in touch. For now, I didn't want to stay with them any longer. I had to remain very careful not to do too much to attract their suspicions.

Thursday 31 October 2002

The day after the verdict, I rang Karim on his mobile to arrange a meeting. We agreed to meet the following day at the time of Friday prayers. That suited my purpose: I wanted to know his friends, the mosques he visited, his activities, in other words, everything about him. Our exchanges during the trial were just an initial approach which, I hoped, would enable me to find out more. I had agreed with Benoît Duquesne and Bruno Ledref, the editor-in-chief and assistant editor-in-chief respectively of the programme *Complément d'enquête*, to do a special programme on Islamism in France. I now had to try to persuade Karim to allow himself to be interviewed on camera by the TV people.

How was I to convince an Islamist, who had already been found guilty of a terrorist offence, to be filmed by a French TV company? I had my speech and my line of argument ready to draw him into the trap which I was preparing for the fundamentalists. Portraying myself as a committed Islamist, I told him that I had suggested to the TV people a feature on 'Muslims persecuted throughout the world for their beliefs'. Naturally I used their own language and phraseology to try to convince him. I insisted that it was possible to bring it off but I needed his help in order to present a 'good image of Muslims'. After some hesitation, Karim ended up accepting my proposal. Naturally I gave him an absolute assurance that his message and probably that of the 'brothers' would be broadcast uncut. 'You're right, Djamel,' he said, 'this too is jihad.'

Our meeting on Friday would allow me to see whether he had changed his mind. I intended to agree the date of the first interview in front of the cameras. I was on sensitive ground, I knew, but I had absolutely nothing to lose. At worst, he would refuse and my plans would fall through.

GOING TO THE NEXT LEVEL

On Friday 1 November, Karim told me that he was intending to
go to pray at the Gallieni Mosque, which is under the Sonacotra
Hostel[1]. I arrived a few minutes late. Karim was waiting patiently
for me, a Quran in his hand. He was reciting verses of the holy
book in a low voice, and hadn't even seen me emerge from the
metro. When I reached him, I didn't want to interrupt his reading. I stopped beside him without saying a word. He sensed
someone's presence and broke off his reading to turn to me,
clearly pleased to see me. Without more ado, we went straight
into the mosque, which was only a short distance away.

When we got there, I experienced a strange feeling: every
time someone looked at me, I thought they recognized me. My

[1]. Translator's note: Sonacotra was founded in 1956 by the French government to provide decent social housing in the period following the
Second World War. It gradually became associated with the provision of
hostel accommodation for the first generation of immigrants from North
Africa.

main fear was that I would find myself in the midst of a group of Islamists who knew my political views, and that would get me lynched. So I had to take the greatest care at every moment and imagine every possible scenario so that I was psychologically prepared for the worst, and especially have an emergency exit or a suitable riposte at the ready. In the prayer room, I realized that I was not yet at the point of needing those; the faithful were listening attentively to a sermon and no one was taking any notice of my presence. I had to overcome my paranoia. I put to one side my thoughts of the worst and made an effort to act as naturally as possible. But to appear natural, I had to *be* natural. I decided to behave like a simple believer who had come to say his prayers and not worry about all the rest. I mustn't try to rush things but let them unfold naturally. That would be how I would behave from now on.

There was nothing shocking in the imam's sermon that day; with Ramadan approaching, he had based it on how a Muslim ought to behave during the holy month. Nonetheless I was beginning to feel uncomfortable because of the suffocating heat in the prayer room. The heating was working at full blast in a packed basement. This was Islam underground. A place of worship is supposed to be somewhere you feel at ease in every sense. It should also fulfil basic health and safety requirements. Psychologically the act of going into a basement to pray strikes me as crazy. That Muslims accept this state of affairs and that the authorities do nothing about such a humiliating situation for France's second religion seems equally crazy. What's more, 'Islam underground' cannot represent true Islam from any point of view.

At around 2 p.m., after the Friday prayers were over, Karim called me over to join him. I followed like a little boy who has been taken to the mosque for the first time. Karim was heading for a group of bearded men. I noticed that my new brother knew lots of people. Karim did the introductions. 'Let me introduce our brother Djamel,' he said to the men. One of them was called Sofiane and another Mourad. I didn't catch the first name of the third man, and I never saw him again. The first man, Sofiane, looked at me with great distrust and scarcely shook my hand, but the other was more polite. After chatting together for a few minutes, we all made to leave. Karim greeted several people we passed on the way. Nearly all of them were rigged out as Islamists.

Outside, Karim excused himself and went off to join a group of four men who looked especially worrying. He left me with Mourad, Sofiane, and the third man. They conversed amongst themselves as if I wasn't there. All three of them were Algerian and, like me, came from the capital. Seeing that they were going to pay me no attention, I decided I had to try to get closer to them. I was standing there like an idiot sharing their uninteresting conversation on the situation in Algeria. I laughed when they laughed and tried to butt in to their discussion, but my new brothers had really decided to ignore me. When I uttered a few words, they looked at me without comment and did no more than nod their heads. I felt as though Karim had been gone for an interminable length of time. The atmosphere was oppressive. I decided then to go on the offensive.

'Which district of Algiers are you from?' I asked innocently.

'Belcourt,' said Sofiane.

'The Casbah,' Mourad answered.

'I was born in Kouba,' I said proudly. This piece of information was not without interest for them. The foundation of the FIS (Islamic Salvation Front), the Algerian Islamist Party, was officially announced in 1989 in the Ibn Badis mosque in Kouba. It was also Ali Benhadj's district. Ali Benhadj[1] was number two in the party which has now been disbanded, and the bridgehead of the Algerian Salafists. What I had come out with, so seemingly innocuous, had relaxed the atmosphere a bit.

I began to talk about the 'Golden Age' of the Algerian Islamist movement, which pleased my 'brothers', who also recalled it with nostalgia. We all talked about 'power which had gone rotten' and 'the inevitable birth of an Islamic state' and all those things that Islamic fundamentalists hold dear. Karim's return brought a halt to this conversation. Sofiane seemed as distrustful as ever; certainly he was taking part in the conversation, but he gave me the impression that he didn't appreciate my presence. He looked at me like I was an intruder and didn't belong here, and he didn't hold back from saying so to Karim. He spoke to him in private a few metres from me, but I clearly heard him exclaim: 'Why are you bringing strangers to us? Who is that man?' Karim replied curtly that if he brought someone with him, he could vouch for him. The exchange between the two of them went no further. While they were talking, I had

1. Ali Benhadj has been imprisoned in the Blida military prison since June 1991. He was condemned to twelve years' imprisonment for having called for jihad in Algeria.

been fiddling with my mobile phone, seemingly indifferent to what they were saying. I had to come across as naive. In other words, I had to play the role of the imbecile who was ready to be manipulated and indoctrinated.

Karim asked Mourad, who was a taxi driver, if he could drop us in Ménilmontant. He said yes. When we were in the car, Sofiane began making comments about Mehdi's reaction at the end of the trial of Bensaïd and Belkacem. I deduced from this that this group must know him. Sofiane was unhappy with Mehdi's attitude. Karim reminded him that Mehdi was extremely young.

'You know how he is. He can't control himself . . .'

Sofiane reminded him of a fundamental rule for all Islamists: 'We are at war, and war is a ruse. You must never show your enemy what you feel or what you plan to do.' And he added, 'If we're going to help them escape from prison, it won't be with kids like him that we'll do it.' I listened without batting an eyelid.

Karim and I got out of the taxi in Ménilmontant. I said lengthy farewells to the others and added, '*Inshallah* [If God wills it] we'll meet again, my brothers.'

I had decided to invite Karim to lunch. He suggested a restaurant in the neighbourhood which served only halal meat and didn't sell alcohol. Karim knew everyone in the restaurant. He introduced me to the owner, Nassreddine, a bearded man who greeted us with a broad smile. He showed us to our table and took our order.

I then began talking to Karim about the TV film which I was planning to make to 'defend the image of Muslims'. Karim repeated to me over and over that I had to defend the cause of jihad through the media. Right in the middle of our conversation, I suddenly noticed at the door two Algerians who used to live in my district of Algiers. I was afraid that they would pounce on me and use my real name, so I made myself as small as possible by drawing my head down into my shoulders and hiding my face with my left hand. Karim looked at me in astonishment. 'What's the matter with you?' he asked.

'I've suddenly got a terrible headache,' I replied, holding my head between my hands. At the same time I cast a quick glance towards the door of the restaurant. What a relief! My two friends had turned tail; the place clearly hadn't been to their taste. So as not to arouse Karim's doubts, I followed through with my act and went to ask the owner of the restaurant if he had any aspirin.

Karim was favourably inclined to take part in my project. Before giving me his final consent, however, he asked if I was sure that my work would not be turned against 'the cause' by the TV channel. I gave him my word. We agreed that the interview would take place the following Tuesday, 5 November, at a hotel in Belleville in Paris. I assured Karim that the TV crew who would be with me would be made up of reliable people who merited his trust. Karim agreed to take part on condition that his face was disguised. We had discussed the film all through the meal. Karim seemed reassured, and his trust in me was growing all the time, which I was pleased about. At the end of lunch we went down to the basement of the restaurant to fulfil the *Asr* (mid-afternoon) prayer. Karim was the one who led the prayer in a small room specially designed for the purpose. We parted at around 3.30 p.m., having agreed to meet again the following Monday.

In the metro I looked around to see if anyone was following me. I would have to take this precaution from now on as I had told Karim that I lived in Montreuil on the outskirts of Paris. Naturally I hadn't been stupid enough to give him the name of the district where I really lived. My new identity was accompanied by a new life which I had created for myself out of nothing. My name was false, my address was false, my life story was false. Everything was false; I was living in a world of falsity and from now on I would have to juggle my double identity.

In the metro I replaced my wedding ring which had been hidden in a pocket in my wallet and I took my watch off my right hand and put it back on my left. Each time I met with my 'brothers' I had to pay attention to this sort of detail. They forbid the wearing of gold because it is prohibited for men of the Muslim religion. As my wedding ring is made of gold, I couldn't let it be seen in front of them. Another detail: most of them wear their watch on their right hand because that is the side of purity, whereas the left side is impure. As time is sacred for them, they prefer to wear their watch on the right. I confess that I sometimes overlooked this detail, without attracting the attention of my 'brothers'.

When I got home I went straight to my computer to make notes on the day and check the information that Karim had given away.

Monday 4 November 2002

I had a meeting arranged with Karim for the evening. The female colleague from France 2, who was working with me on the film, came with me. I made the introductions. Karim wanted to meet her before the interview arranged for the following day. At the agreed time he was waiting for us, smiling as usual, at the exit of the Couronnes metro station. Almost as soon as he had shaken my hand, he reminded me that he didn't touch women's hands. My 'brother' then told me that he would like to buy some oriental cakes for my colleague, as he wanted to make a good impression. He went to a nearby shop and asked for a kilo of *mekroud*, honey cakes which are highly valued in North Africa. His attitude was false and hypocritical: while he was making a show of great hospitality towards my colleague, he was whispering to me that 'you always have to give a warm welcome to infidels'. He asked me later if it might be possible to try to convert her to Islam. He even suggested putting her in touch with 'sisters who had converted' so that they would influence her in the right direction.

Karim invited us to go to a café nearby, and we began our conversation there over a cup of green tea. He spoke to us about the Muslim religion for over an hour. He also talked about jihad, in an attempt to justify the unjustifiable. Nevertheless, he remained wary. He was watching what he said so as not to shock my colleague. In the course of this discussion, Karim spoke again about Djamel Hervé Loiseau and Brahim Yadel, two Frenchmen, the first found dead of hypothermia in the Tora-Bora mountains in Afghanistan, and the other held at the American base in Guantanamo Bay. Both of them had gone to take part in jihad in distant countries and had been trained in Osama Bin Laden's camps. Their ideological training – in other words their indoctrination – had been carried out by Karim and other brothers, who continued to give their 'classes in religion' in the Omar and Abu-Bakr mosques, both situated in Belleville. Karim also talked about his 'attachment' to the Palestinian, Afghan and Chechen causes and expressed his hatred for the Americans and the Jews. His language was naturally that of an Islamist, but he moderated it a bit, toning down certain aspects so as not to shock my colleague (as he told me later) whom he was meeting for the first time. The whole way through the film we made with him, he unfailingly engaged in this double-speak. The first discourse was intended for me, and captured what was really in his heart, allowing a fascist, war-mongering, hate-filled side to appear, in which the negation of other people was a constant. The second, intended for 'the infidels', was smoothed out with tolerance, understanding and respect. Karim didn't infringe the rule followed by Islamists the world over, whether they are self-proclaimed 'moderates' or 'radicals'. They all employ manipulation and 'twin-track' language. It is what they call *takiya*. I had at last the chance to see this truth for myself. I was experiencing it in action.

At the end of this long conversation, Karim agreed to be

interviewed. We agreed to meet the next day, as arranged, in a hotel nearby. We had decided to rent a hotel room for the day so that the interview could take place in complete privacy. We parted company at around 9 p.m. . . .

Tuesday 5 November 2002

At 10 a.m. I turned up as arranged near the Couronnes metro station opposite the Abu-Bakr mosque. The France 2 team had rented the hotel room and were busy setting up their equipment. It was market day and also the last day before the start of Ramadan, and there was a huge number of people in the area. Opposite me were two people, one young and one old, brandishing a sign asking passers-by to give contributions to the building of a mosque in the suburbs. Beside them, another even younger, bearded man was selling Muslim calendars, distributed by the Habashat, a sort of Islamist sect whose principal mission is to oppose Wahabism, by putting forward its own erroneous reading of the Muslim religion. I looked at this circus and asked myself what could push Muslims to so many divergent viewpoints. Islam today includes a multitude of currents, each of them claiming to possess the supreme truth. This is a fact made easier by the intellectual failure of almost all theologians who, if they do not actually preach extremism of one form or another, keep quiet, mostly out of cowardice.

Some policemen interrupted my thoughts. They were checking the papers of the two men who had been asking for money. 'We belong to an association,' they insisted, flourishing a sheaf of documents. In a few minutes the check was over and the two men were able to get back to their appeal. What would the money be used for? To build a mosque? I doubt we'll ever know.

At last Karim turned up. He was a few minutes late but that didn't bother me as I had not had time to get bored. My 'brother', red-eyed, was clearly lacking sleep. After the usual greetings, I asked him to come with me to the hotel where we were going to record the interview. But first, I wanted to buy a few bottles of mineral water, so naturally I went towards the first grocer's we came to.

'No, no, Djamel, not here!' exclaimed Karim.

'Why?'

'Can't you see they're Jews?'

I had forgotten this detail: Islamists never buy from Jewish shopkeepers, though they know very well, let it be said in passing, that the Prophet himself traded with Jews in Medina.

To justify myself to Karim, I said, 'Ah yes, I hadn't noticed that, brother!'

The France 2 crew had everything ready so that the recording could begin. The interview lasted over three hours. Right at the start, Karim was asked about the reasons for his arrest on 26 May 1998, before the World Cup.

'It was a terrible judicial mistake!' he told us, adding that he had been doing nothing wrong; he was simply in possession of duplicated copies of Islamist literature and had been giving classes in the mosques. The classes were, in reality, indoctrination sessions in which young men like Loiseau and Yadel took part. As for the copies, they were communiques from the Algerian GSPC, the Salafist group directed by Hassan Hattab.[1] Karim was

1. Hassan Hattab is the head of the GSPC. He broke away from the GIA.

responsible for distributing them in France and throughout Europe. The texts contained calls for assassinations but also directions intended for GSPC cells active in mainland Europe. In 1998 the GSPC pledged its allegiance to Osama Bin Laden's Al Qaeda, and Bin Laden sent a Yemeni emissary Hassan Hattab to coordinate the actions of the two terrorist organizations.

In front of the France 2 camera, Karim played down his own importance and portrayed himself as a victim who had suffered 'an enormous injustice'. Nevertheless, he didn't hide his support for Bin Laden's projects and used all his sophistry to justify his actions, especially the attacks of 11 September, which struck him as 'legitimate'. According to him, only Bin Laden and the Taliban followed an authentic form of Islam; all other Muslims should consequently be fought against, including the Saudi regime. As for the threat to France, Karim responded more subtly and gave us to believe that there was absolutely no risk that France would become victim of a terrorist attack, claims which were completely at odds with what he told me in private.

Karim made some surprising revelations on camera. 'When Algeria or Tunisia become Islamic states, we shan't sit and twiddle our thumbs. We'll propose Islam to Jacques Chirac or Tony Blair. And if they don't accept Islam, we'll do it by conquest,' he said, revealing the true aims of the Islamists. 'The whole world must be governed by Allah's word,' he added. These words echoed those of Djamel Zitouni, the leader of the GIA in 1995,

In particular he is opposed to the massacres of the civilian population ordered by the leaders of the GIA groups, who are behind dozens of massacres in Algeria.

who had, let us not forget, invited the French President to convert to Islam just a few months before the beginning of the wave of attacks on France.

After this long interview, we decided to go and have lunch at Nassreddine's, the restaurateur who supported the Islamist doctrine. There we continued our discussion of Islam. We were about to start eating when I saw Mourad, the taxi driver I'd met at Friday prayers, suddenly come into the restaurant. I got up at once to say hello to him. He sat down at our table and told me that he'd heard from Karim that we'd gone to the same school in Algiers.

'I was at the Emir-Abdelkader *lycée*, too,' he said, but unlike Karim, he didn't remember me. As if to check me out, he asked me to remind him of the names of the headmaster and some of the teachers. I did this without hesitation, and Mourad seemed reassured by my responses. I had just forgotten the name of the head supervisor, but I gave him such a precise description Mourad ended up giving me his name. He went on to question me on former FIS officers. Having presented myself as a former activist in the Islamist party, I had to give him good answers here too. I decided to list all those whose names I knew, most of whom had died after joining the Resistance. I passed yet another test.

I explained that I had withdrawn from the Islamist movement following the suspension of the electoral process in Algeria in 1992 because I had lost confidence in several former members of the party. I emphasized that my problem with the Algerian authorities was due to my religious and political beliefs. I had in fact adopted the history of an Islamist militant who hadn't had a very significant career, but who was convinced by the principle of jihad, while remaining very careful not to get arrested. Karim listened attentively. He and Mourad gave the impression that they believed my story. I had told them just enough to be credible. I noticed as the days went by that my new 'brothers' trusted me more and more.

At the end of the meal we went down into the restaurant's basement to pray. There, Karim asked me what I thought of the interview. 'You did well, brother,' I said. He was happy and reassured but suggested I select the words which would be broadcast very carefully. I reminded him of my personal devotion to 'the cause', which pleased him.

'You know, Djamel, what you're doing in your work is also jihad,' he said. I showed him that I was very happy to hear that.

'Really?'

'Absolutely,' he insisted, reciting a verse from the Quran.

To Karim, I was as worthy as those who committed attacks.

'Listen, Djamel, the enemy attacks us with his weapons, his journalists, his intellectuals, and his TV stations, so we must do the same . . .'

After this brief discussion, we returned to join the crew, though not before reciting our prayers. We didn't remain together much longer; around 4 p.m. we went our separate ways, having made an appointment for the following day. In fact, Karim had suggested that I take his classes in religion. He asked me to buy a notebook so that I could learn the dogma and principles of jihad. I promised him that I would devote the month of Ramadan to taking his classes.

Wednesday 6 November 2002

First day of Ramadan. That day I had a lot of work to do and I found an excuse to avoid Karim, who wanted me to start the classes in religion at the mosque. I left a message on his mobile and spent the day preparing an article for the weekly paper, *Marianne*.

A team from Canal Plus had made a documentary in which they tried to show that the attacks in France in 1995 were not the work of Islamists, but of the Algerian secret service, acting with the complicity of the French secret service. This was insane to the point of wilfulness. For a number of years, there has been a trend in France to attempt to clear the Islamists of blame for their crimes. Even where the events of 11 September are concerned, there have been 'enlightened minds' who have maintained, in a terrible deception, that these attacks which changed the face of the world were carried out by the American secret service.

Over several months I made a point of questioning the Islamists I came into contact with about this type of claim. Karim, who was very close to the two men accused of the 1995 attacks, Boualem Bensaïd and Smaïn Aït Ali Belkacem, told me categorically that those two Islamists came specially from the Algerian resistance to assassinate imam Sahraoui and to perpetrate the attacks on French soil. He added that they were both close to Djamel Zitouni and had pledged allegiance to death to him. I asked him if Zitouni could be an agent of the Algerian secret service.

'Impossible,' he said, explaining, 'Zitouni certainly went astray during the jihad by killing brothers who had been great fighters, but he never worked with the regime. What people say about him is untrue.' Karim also added that 'those who decided at that time to strike France had made a mistake both strategically and from the point of view of dogma'. In his opinion, even the choice of target, in this case the metro, was 'an error'.

Karim, who never hid his membership of the GSPC from me, told me that he was keen to convince the brothers of the GIA in prison in France to swear allegiance to Hassan Hattab. He was all the more credible in this as he didn't have any lingering affection for the former GIA leaders, Djamel Zitouni and Antar Zouabri. He had every reason to run them down, but he didn't do so. He made do with repeating to me that the GIA and its leaders had taken a wrong path and followed the wrong strategy, which, in his opinion, 'had done a lot of harm to the cause'.

As for the book[1] which suggested that Bin Laden and Islamists were not behind the attacks of 11 September, Karim replied on camera that it was indeed 'the sheikh' [Osama Bin Laden] who 'carried out the attacks, and that the brothers are capable of that sort of operation and even more than that'.

According to him, these claims which try to exculpate the Islamists are the work of people who want to play down the

---

1. *L'effroyable imposture*, Thierry Meyssan (Carnot, 2002)

abilities and intelligence of Muslims to carry out jihad. In what he said, Karim confirmed for me something which I have always thought about certain sections of the media: even though the Islamists claim responsibility for their crimes, it's a sad fact that a certain element on the far left doggedly try to clear them of blame.

After I finished my article for *Marianne*, I decided to call Karim back, as he hadn't tried to ring me since I left a message for him on his mobile. My second call was no more fruitful. I left another message and waited all day in vain. Karim seemed to be unreachable by phone. After the end of the fast, my telephone rang at last. It was Karim. He told me in a weary voice that he had had a road accident; he had been knocked off the scooter by a car. I asked if he needed anything and told him I'd like to visit him the following day. He accepted.

In fact, I had invited myself to his flat to check the truth of his story. We agreed to meet after the end of the fast. I took advantage of the chance to tell him that I would bring a video of the programme Canal Plus broadcast, clearing the Islamists of blame for the 1995 attacks. I was interested to see how he would react to the assertions in this pseudo-investigation. In addition, I wanted to learn more about him from his environment.

Thursday 7 November 2002

After the end of the fast, I was in a café near my home having a cigarette and coffee. I was about to enter the wolf's lair and needed to concentrate so as not to take any unnecessary risks. I had left all my own papers at home and only had a new season ticket with me, bearing my false name and an old identity photograph. As usual, I had taken off my wedding ring and put my watch on my right hand. I hadn't shaved in over a month and I was beginning to look like my 'brothers'.

When I got to Ménilmontant, I called Karim on his mobile to tell him that I was in his neighbourhood. We had arranged that I would do this so that he could give me the entry code for his building. I got his answering machine. That put me on edge as I was really keen that nothing should go wrong. I had to control everything, try to anticipate everything. That strategy would allow me to avoid dangerous situations. I decided to calm down and went to buy some cakes for Karim. I kept my mobile in my hand and waited for it to ring. Karim rang half an hour later. He apologized and gave me his entry code, adding, 'It's on the third floor, on the left.'

As I went up the stairs, my heart was beating frantically. I knew there were other Islamists in his apartment, and each time we met I was afraid that I would come face to face with someone who recognized me. When I reached the third floor, I tried to control my breathing. Karim opened the door. He had indeed been injured. He was limping and had an enormous bandage covering his leg from knee to ankle. I tried to show how concerned about him I'd been, and I asked how the accident had happened. He thanked me for the cakes and asked me to come in. I quickly looked into the apartment. At the end of the hall, I immediately recognized Mourad and Sofiane. There was also a third, younger, man there. I later discovered that he was Karim's brother-in-law. I greeted the three men warmly as I went into the living room. It was a nice, well-decorated apartment: luxurious for a former prisoner with no job!

Karim started to explain to me how his accident had happened, but his story was interrupted by Mourad, who said that he and Sofiane had to go. Karim said, 'I hope you haven't forgotten our brothers in prison.'

Each man took a large envelope out of his pocket and handed it to Karim. He then turned to me: 'Djamel, you must help to collect money for the brothers in prison, too.'

'Of course,' I said. He'd have a long wait, though, before he saw me giving money to terrorists!

I had just identified one of Karim's clandestine activities: he acted as a central collection point for some of the money for the 'cause'. That enabled him to pay for the needs of Islamist prisoners such as Boualem Bensaïd, Smaïn Aït Ali Belkacem, Kamel Daoudi, Adel Machat and so on, all of whom had been convicted of terrorist offences. I didn't know how the money they collected was shared out, but I was to learn more as my investigation went on.

Karim explained that I should contact all the people I knew

and ask them for money. He even stipulated the way in which I should do it: 'If they are brothers, tell them it's for the prisoners. And if they are infidels, tell them the money will go to the poor.'

Karim's brother-in-law decided to leave at the same time as Mourad and Sofiane. All three said goodbye with *Asslam-o-Alaikum* [Peace be upon you].

In the gloom, I could make out two shadowy figures in chadors. Karim told me that they were his wife and a convert to Islam whose Algerian husband had been imprisoned for a terrorist offence. I asked Karim to introduce me so that I could 'collect their stories'. He refused, claiming that the husband of the convert had forbidden his wife to 'speak to the media'. So that was all I would find out about her . . .

As I was now alone with Karim, I suggested that we watch the Canal Plus programme. He went straight to the VCR and put the cassette in. The 'documentary' had only just begun when he grimaced.

'They're liars!' he said, stopping the video. He was so disgusted he didn't want to watch any more. What had annoyed him was an interview in which it was claimed that Djamel Zitouni was a homosexual.

I decided to change the subject and shift the conversation on to Bin Laden, the 'holy war', and religion in general. I sensed he was on his guard. He was talkative, but remained wary as far as his activities and his plans were concerned. It was still too soon. Karim, however, didn't hold back from putting lots of questions to me. He seemed especially interested in information about Dalil Boubakeur, the rector of the Paris mosque, and Soheïb

Bencheikh, the rector of Marseilles. In 1998, the network to which Karim belonged had already been making plans to assassinate Dalil Boubakeur. According to Karim, the murder of the two rectors would be 'legitimate' because they had been judged 'infidels' by the Saudi theologians Karim and the other brothers were in contact with. He also wanted me to get information on prominent Algerian figures, especially if they were on non-official visits to France, and on Algerian diplomats posted to Paris. The detail of these questions was intriguing. What were they planning?

After a long conversation, I decided to go home. It was late and I didn't want to stay any longer. On my way back, I went over in my mind everything I had just seen and heard. As the days and weeks went by, my conviction became stronger. I was associating with GSPC activists who defended the cause of Al Qaeda. It was clear, however, that the members of this cell were not 'operationals'. Nonetheless, the task of Karim and the other brothers was to look after all the logistical aspects which precede and follow terrorist operations. Their role was to gather information, collect money, and preach the cause so as to indoctrinate new recruits. They probably engaged in other activities which I hadn't yet discovered.

Karim was obviously the network coordinator. He knew everyone, he collected the money, carried out religious teaching, acted as go-between, welcomed brothers when they were passing through Paris, found them inconspicuous places to stay, got hold of false papers – all necessary support for operational cells.

From then on, I was convinced that I was associating not just with Islamists, but with members of a terrorist cell. The terrorist is not only the person who places the bomb but also the person who hides him, gives him information and puts at his disposal the life-blood of war – money.

Karim and I had agreed that we would call each other regularly, but the next day I didn't contact him. I wanted to put a bit of distance between myself and all of this, and think over what I had experienced during the past month and a half. I had to concentrate on what I had to do and say to the brothers in order to preserve my safety and not arouse their suspicions. Karim had asked me to do a lot of things and up till then I had done absolutely nothing. He had specifically given me the mission of collecting money and bringing him information about prominent figures. I had to come up with arguments which would justify my lack of results, while still holding out the prospect of certain things. I thought about subjects on which I could misinform them to test what they were really capable of. But that would be dangerous and I couldn't undertake anything illegal. It was clear that I wasn't going to fall into my own trap.

After a day of reflection, I decided to manage events from day to day, giving them false information on general subjects, for example, that Bin Laden was going to appear on Al Jazeera soon . . .

Saturday 9 November 2002

I had a meeting around 3 p.m. near the Hotel de Ville in Paris with a journalist friend I hadn't seen for a long time. I was on my way there when my phone rang. It was Karim.

'*Asslam-o-Alaikum*, Djamel, can you come to the mosque on the rue Polonceau? I'm meeting some other brothers there.'

'I'll be there in half an hour.'

Within a minute I had cancelled my meeting and hailed a taxi. In the taxi, I went through my ritual of taking off my wedding ring and putting my watch on my right hand. The astonished taxi driver watched me in his mirror, but didn't say anything. This meeting had not been planned and that worried me a bit. I was carrying my own identity papers, which I distributed among the various pockets in my briefcase.

The taxi driver dropped me at the boulevard Barbès, in the heart of the 18th *arrondissement*. From there it was just a few metres to the rue Polonceau. When I got to the mosque, the *Al-Asr* prayer had just begun. From afar, I caught sight of Sofiane, who came running up. He greeted me quickly and pointed out that we were late. We both went into the mosque quickly and took our places alongside the faithful. At the end of the prayer I had an idea: I told Sofiane that someone had just stolen my wallet. He began to look for it with me. He was outraged that someone could have taken it while I was praying. This piece of subterfuge, I hoped, would allow me to get myself out of a difficult situation if I was subjected to an identity card check in their presence for some reason or another.

While I was discussing the loss of my identity papers with Sofiane, Mourad arrived at the mosque. He greeted us, went off to pray alone, and then returned. Sofiane reported the 'incident' to him and he seemed equally shocked by what had happened. Karim still hadn't arrived. I asked about him, but no one had seen him. People said that he was bound to come as Sheikh Salaheddine, a fundamentalist imam, had been due to preach, though this had been cancelled at the last moment. We stayed at the mosque for nearly an hour making small talk. Finally Karim rang me to apologize for not having been able to come. Was this another test to see if he could count on me when he called or had he asked someone to observe me from a distance to check my story? I shall never know, but what is certain is that Karim didn't change his attitude to me.

I took advantage of the moment to tell him that my wallet had been stolen in the mosque. He suggested that I report it, but not tell the police that the theft took place in the mosque, as that 'would damage the image of Islam and the brothers in the eyes of the infidel'.

I told Mourad and Sofiane what Karim had advised on the phone. 'He's right,' they agreed. I told them that I would come back and report the theft after the end of the fast. I justified my decision on the grounds that I didn't want to risk being held up for a long time in the police station. The two brothers thought that sensible.

Mourad asked me what direction I was going in.

'Home to Montreuil.'

'That's lucky! We live there too. We'll come with you.'

I stayed calm and accepted his suggestion with warm thanks. I didn't have any choice: a Muslim must return home on a Saturday afternoon half an hour before the end of the fast. I couldn't find an excuse for not following them. When we were in the car, I thought about the address in Montreuil I would give them. I decided on a small apartment building near the rue la Croix-de-Chavaux, not far from the mosque. From then on, this would be my address. On the way there, the two brothers asked me questions about Algeria, my studies, my career and my political activities. I answered all their questions confidently. I had learned my new history by heart and there was no chance they would beat me at that game. After a few minutes they exchanged glances, clearly convinced by my answers.

When we got to Montreuil, I told them which road to take to 'my place' without a moment's hesitation. We were five minutes from the end of the fast and they were in a hurry to get home. With great confidence I pointed out the building I lived in. I even invited them to come in and eat with me at home. Fortunately they refused. I confess that on the spur of the moment, I had pushed things a bit far, but I had to take a risk like that to stay credible.

We said goodbye quickly and wished each other 'bon appétit'. I got out of the car, and gave them a final wave as Mourad was doing a U-turn. According to what they had said, they lived on a housing estate about two kilometres from where they had dropped me off. I walked on for a moment, looking around as I went. At the corner I quickly disappeared into a taxi, which would take me to my real home. I had just won another day and that gave me a certain satisfaction, which was all the greater as I could see I was gaining more and more of my new brothers' confidence. I decided nonetheless not to see them for a few days to try to recover some sense of normality. I needed a break. Not a moment had gone by when I wasn't thinking of them. I couldn't help asking myself a host of questions. Were they planning something? Were they investigating me? Were they or their accomplices ready to go into action?

During the days that followed, Karim called me regularly. Each time I told him I was extremely busy with the report I was preparing on the Muslims. He questioned me to find out whether I was following religious observance scrupulously during the month of Ramadan. He never brought up sensitive subjects on the phone. Any time he wanted to talk to me about something important, he would arrange a meeting. I reassured him on the score of my 'religious observance' and we agreed to meet again very soon.

Monday 18 November 2002

Appointment with Karim in Ménilmontant. I decided I would talk to him about Imad, alias Omar Saiki, who in 1998 was regarded by the French authorities as the head of his group.

We had arranged to meet near the entrance to the metro after the end of the fast, as Ramadan dictated. I had been waiting for some time when he arrived. He was walking with crutches because of his accident. We headed straight for a café he particularly liked. As usual, Karim talked about religion, the Prophet, conquests, and jihad in order to complete my ideological training.

He advised me to follow the Saudi *oulemas* who preach Wahabism and Salafism.[1] In their view, a Muslim who does not pray is not a Muslim, likewise a woman who does not wear the veil, and all those who do not conform to the precepts of Wahabism rather than Islam. Karim and other brothers are the purest products of Wahabism; their obscurantism offers sufficient proof of that.

Having discussed religious subjects with him, I asked Karim for news of Omar Saiki. At first he replied evasively, but when I

1. *Oulemas* is the plural of *alem*, which means 'Muslim theologian'. *Wahabism* is the doctrine founded by Mohamed Ibn Abdelwaheb, which preaches a hardline version of Islam. Wahabism is spread from its base in Saudi Arabia. *Salafism* is from the root, *salaf*, which literally means 'ancestor'. Salafists preach a return to the origins of Islam.

persisted, he told me Saiki's story in more detail, which allowed me to compare his version with information I already possessed.

Saiki used to give 'classes in religion' and it was obvious that the profile of him that Karim sketched for me corresponded perfectly to what I expected. Omar Saiki was the representative, or at the very least one of the representatives, of the GSPC on the continent of Europe. He evidently was in frequent contact with the other cells in Europe, and was as familiar with the Islamists in Germany and Great Britain as with those in France and Italy.

However, his career was fairly atypical. When Saiki was exiled from Algeria in the early 1990s, he was in no sense of the word an Islamist. Several witnesses confirmed to me that he went to bars and frequented prostitutes more often than he attended the mosque or went to listen to Abu Qatada's sermons. Saiki's profile was typical of those who have landed up in the Islamist movement by 'accident' and whose zeal redoubles when they find themselves in terrorist cells which provide them with a remedy for the frustrations felt by a whole group of young North African men. Having learned to repeat some half-baked theological ideas, Saiki styled himself Professor of Theology and began to contaminate other young people similarly.

The picture of Saiki which Karim was painting for me glossed over the exact role he played. He listed all his boss's qualities for me – he presented him as 'enterprising', 'dynamic', and 'committed' – but not without allowing a certain jealousy to show through. Stripped of his French citizenship in September 2002,

Saiki took refuge in London to escape possible expulsion to Algeria. I asked Karim if he could put me in touch with him and he promised to do the necessary to arrange a meeting.

We stayed together till midnight, when Karim offered to drive me home in his car. I didn't know that he owned a car, and I would never have suspected that he would be able to drive after his scooter accident. I tried to dissuade him, but he was so insistent that I ended up accepting his offer. Naturally he was planning to drive me to Montreuil. This didn't put him out at all, as he was not intending to spend the night at home. Active Islamists avoid spending Monday and Thursday nights at home. In their view, the police are likeliest to take them in for questioning and carry out house searches after 6 a.m. on Tuesday and Friday mornings. This claim struck me as ridiculous at first, but after checking it out, I can report that it is not entirely without substance. It clearly satisfies the police and magistrates' desire for administrative order. I realized that the Islamists are sometimes well informed.

Karim told me on the way that he had at his disposal several 'safe houses', one of which was in the Barbès district and another in Montreuil. He proudly showed me several bunches of keys, and added, 'Djamel, if you ever need to go into hiding, there won't be any problem.'

I smiled in spite of myself at this, as if I ever had to go into hiding, it would undoubtedly be to escape him or his brothers.

In Montreuil, Karim headed towards the mosque, which was natural as he knew that I lived in that district. As he got close to my so-called home, I noticed a group of young people near the entrance of the building. I asked Karim to set me down a few dozen metres away, but he obstinately insisted on taking me right to the door. I didn't have any option. The most important thing was to avoid panicking. I managed to stay calm as he stopped the car near the group of youths. He probably wanted to reassure himself that I was really going to go into the building. I had the feeling that I was done for – he was about to discover my deception.

But I said goodnight to him warmly. The youths were looking at me strangely. Seeing two bearded men outside their building at 1 a.m. was fairly unusual. As I got out of the car I had a flash of inspiration: I went up to the group of youths and began greeting them one by one, with Karim watching me as he put the car into reverse. This was how I would prove to him that these young people were from my neighbourhood. There were about ten of them staring at me with vacant expressions. They couldn't understand why I would be shaking their hands when they had never seen me before in their lives.

This manoeuvre allowed me to gain some time; Karim was already back on the main street. I gave him a final wave before disappearing into the building. Then one of the youths called out to me, asking who I was and where I was going. I came back outside and gave him the first name that came into my head. They all answered together that no one of that name lived there. They were still eyeing me distrustfully. To reassure them, I asked them for the rue du général Gallieni.

'It's over on the other side,' one of them replied. As I left, I heard one of them say to the others, 'He must be a nutcase.' And perhaps he wasn't completely wrong; to do what I was doing you would have to have a screw or two loose somewhere.

When I reached the main street I looked left. Karim was far in the distance: I could make out his car waiting at a red light at the end of the rue de la Croix-de-Chavaux. I ran towards the taxi rank, but before I got to it, I saw a taxi dropping off a fare, and I got in without even asking the driver if he was free. I must have appeared highly suspicious, but the driver didn't make any comment. By the time I got home, it was nearly 2 a.m.

WITH MEMBERS OF AL QAEDA

Tuesday 19 November 2002

I decided to film Karim with a hidden camera. I wanted him to repeat views he had already expressed to me so that I could put them in the documentary for France 2.

Karim for his part was keen to see me because he wanted to do another interview on the subject of jihad; he felt that he had not been sufficiently precise in the first interview we had recorded. This time we had a meeting before the end of the fast at 3:30 p.m.

As usual, he welcomed me with a large smile. I suggested that we sat down somewhere and he pointed to a bench. Without any preamble, I tackled the subject we had discussed before: the choice of targets. I had noticed that Karim, like the terrorists of the GSPC, didn't agree with targeting civilians directly. In fact, he often criticized the action taken by Djamel Zitouni's men in 1995 in targeting the metro and other public places. I asked him to explain to me how a target could be identified. In addition, I wanted him to explain it to me from the point of view of their ideology. Even if it was somewhat ambiguous, his answer shed light on the logic of Islamists loyal to Osama Bin Laden.

According to Karim, 'When a bomb is placed in the metro, the people are targeted. On the other hand, if it is placed in the Eiffel Tower, it's the *symbol* which is targeted, even if members of the public happen to lose their lives.' He concluded his answer with the sentence: 'We should attack symbols, not civilians. Sheikh Osama wasn't aiming at the civilians who were inside the World Trade Centre, but the symbol represented by the Twin Towers.'

I asked him next about the risks which threatened France. From Karim's point of view, France could be the target of terrorist operations if 'it sides too closely with the Americans, especially if there's a war against Iraq and Muslims'. He continued his analysis, stating that, 'The sheikh [Osama Bin Laden] could strike France just as he struck Bali.'

Then we moved on to a discussion about the leader of Al Qaeda.

'Do you think that many Muslims agree with Bin Laden's actions?'

'All those who are sincere with Allah support Osama Bin Laden. Any Muslim who doesn't love Bin Laden has hypocrisy in his heart. There are certainly people who criticize him, but those people haven't given us any alternative . . .'

In the middle of our discussion, Karim asked me again for further commitment to them.

'How can I help you?'

'You know what needs to be done.'

'Tell me exactly what you expect of me.'

'I've told you, Djamel, that every Muslim must help us.'

'But I am talking about *me*, Karim. What exactly do you expect of *me*?'

'Listen to me carefully, Djamel. The Prophet said: "Allah has made easy the task of each of us." You are made to do journalism. Do your job in a way that serves the cause. You can help us as a journalist.'

'You want me to do propaganda?'

'*Barak Allahou Fik* [May God bless you]. Try to show the actions of Al Qaeda in a positive light. In an indirect and subtle way, explain the reasons that drive Al Qaeda to proclaim jihad. Cite the injustice which Muslims suffer throughout the world . . . you know what to do . . . above all, you must do it intelligently . . .'

'And apart from that, what else can I do?'

'If you come across people who have a lot of money, suggest that they help us. Money is very important. You must keep in mind that a bullet today costs 22 Francs.'

I had just been officially recruited by Karim. I was experiencing a very important moment. He must have had great confidence in me. I pushed him to say more. Karim began by revealing that he considered himself to be 'a Muslim terrorist'. With a smile, he recited a verse of the Quran to me which says, in substance, 'Prepare what force you can and cavalry to terrorize the enemies of God and your enemies.'

Then he went on to talk about Djamel Hervé Loiseau. He

confirmed that he was the person who had indoctrinated Loiseau, and added, 'Now that he has died a martyr, I am nothing compared to him.'

I decided to provoke him: 'Why haven't you gone to take part in the jihad ?'

'It was the theologians who stopped me. They said to me, "You have mastered two languages [Arabic and French]; you must stay in France" . . .'

'But why do they want you to stay in France? Do you have a specific role?'

'Well . . . I . . . I stir people up . . . I encourage them to join the jihad. It's important for Islam . . .'

Karim had just confirmed my suspicions in front of my hidden camera. I was delighted. I had his admission, his incontrovertible statement which clarified his exact role beyond any shadow of doubt. It was indeed he and others who had 'incited' a young man like Djamel Hervé Loiseau to go and die in the Afghan mountains. It was his fault, and that of his brothers, that mixed-up people found themselves signed up and setting off for struggles which were not theirs. I had in front of me one of the bosses. He produced the cannon fodder for international terrorism. Here was someone who held a French identity card, whose objective was to lure young people away from their families to send them to Afghanistan, Chechnya or elsewhere. I wanted to spit in his face or punch him, but I checked my anger and held my revulsion at bay. He disgusted me all the more as he remained in France, collecting money without working, stuffing himself from morning till night, while encouraging kids to go and get killed thousands of miles from home. Moreover, he didn't hesitate to play his role to the hilt when I led him to believe that I too was thinking about going to join the jihad.

'Go, Djamel. And don't worry about your wife and children. God will protect them.'

He explained that I would have to go to be trained in Chechnya first. I decided to take advantage of his talkativeness to glean other information, to work out his role, and to identify his contacts.

'You were talking just then about theologians. But who really prevented you from going?'

'It was sheikh Selmane.'

'Who's sheikh Selmane?'

'What? You don't know who he is? The Saudi sheikh Selmane Al'Ouda. You know, the fifteen Saudis of 11 September were all trained by him . . .'

Of course I knew Selmane Al'Ouda by reputation but I wanted Karim to tell me what he knew about him. Sheikh Selmane is currently one of the most important Saudi ideologues; a prophet of Wahabism, he is notable for declaring suicide missions (which he terms 'martyr operations') to be legitimate. The Salafists almost all have a direct telephone link to him and consult him before any important decision. He was arrested by the Saudi authorities in the early 1990s for calling for popular opposition to the royal family, and was released in 1999, since when he has taken up his activities again. He is one of the people who support Bin Laden's terrorist activities and give them a religious justification.

73

I was curious to know which camp they would have gone to for training before the events of 11 September.

'Al Farouk camp, Osama's camp . . . that was where brothers Djamel [Hervé Loiseau] and Ibrahim [Yadel] were trained.'

'And did you know the channels to get there?'

'Of course! I knew the whole thing. And as I said, I would have gone there myself if it hadn't been for sheikh Semane's directives.'

'If you had gone, you would be a real operational today. Has your cover been blown since you were arrested in 1998?'

'That's right, my cover's blown. That's why I wear a beard now. But don't worry, Djamel, lots of our brothers are unknown to the police. You'll see them in the streets: they're clean-shaven and even wear an earring. You'd never guess that they are mujahidin. You'd take them for boys from nice families.'

Karim ended this sentence with a jubilant laugh which gave me a cold sweat. In the course of the same conversation I learned that a brother who had gone to take part in the jihad in Chechnya had just returned to France. According to Karim, the brother in question had been very well trained over there and was supposed to be going back after a 'mission' in Europe. He didn't tell me any more about it. By a 'mission' did he mean an act of terrorism which was being prepared? I didn't get any further details to convince me of the credibility of this information, at least not that day.

What he said squared with all the hypotheses put forward by most of the people who work on this subject, and confirmed all the information I had been able to gather during the past few years. Islamist terrorism still has long years ahead of it: it demands swift and decisive action. That is the least I can say.

After an hour with Karim, I decided to go home. I had heard enough for today. In fact, I was in quite a state. This operation was beginning to get to me mentally. It was becoming more and more difficult: I was in contact with people I have always fought against and whose opinions disgusted me. Nonetheless, I had to continue to the end, and I had to explore every little detail which being close to them permitted, so as to understand how they functioned and how they reacted. I had to discover their short-term and medium-term aims. I was like a man who had encountered extra-terrestrials and had asked them to take him to their planet; I wanted to travel for as long as possible in their galaxy. I was trying to penetrate the mystery which surrounds the activities of the Islamo-terrorist movement, and I would therefore leave my own feelings to one side and pursue my quest. However, I set myself a limit: I decided to stop by 15 January 2003 at the latest. So I still had a month and a half to spend in their crazy world.

All that evening and all the next day I kept going back over what Karim had revealed. I couldn't stop myself thinking about the discussion we had had. He acted in accordance with the wishes of individuals who lived in Saudi Arabia, Great Britain and elsewhere. At the time of his arrest in 1998, this Algerian, who was naturalized as a French citizen in 2000, had a mission to send young Muslims living in France to get killed abroad. Confronted with acts such as these, the law is clearly powerless.

It's not my place to give my views on the laws which are

currently in force, and I don't know if the risks I took will serve any purpose. What I do know, however, is that I acted in accordance with my conscience to try first to contribute to saving innocent lives, and second, to reveal my experience to the public so that they can judge for themselves the dangers which threaten our democracy. I insist on this point in order to respond in advance to those right-thinking people who claim to have understood the phenomenon of Islamism from the comfort of their offices in Paris. I'm talking particularly about the elements of the far left in France which tries, through the abuse of arguments based on 'human rights', to scupper any action which denounces Islamism as an ideology and excuses those same Islamists for the crimes they continue to commit throughout the world.

For the sake of truth, I have to add here that Karim Bourti, whose words I have been relating, is represented by Patrick Baudoin, a lawyer who was formerly head of a well known NGO and who is very active in the field of human rights. Will he continue to defend Bourti? I don't entertain any illusions to the contrary. I believe that ultimately the differences I have with people like him are due to the fact that we have different conceptions not of human rights but of humanity itself.

Thursday 21 November 2002

Karim had told me about a free restaurant which one of his Islamist friends had opened in Barbès during the month of Ramadan. He had suggested I bring along the France 2 cameras so that TV viewers could see 'Muslims' charitable work'. I was making my way there at around 3 p.m., when my mobile rang. It was Karim: 'Where are you, Djamel? It's time for prayers.'

'I'm in Barbès. I've just got off the metro.'

'Hurry up, I'm waiting for you with the brothers.'

Karim now considered me one of his men. His tone with me had changed. He still spoke to me with respect, but he gave me instructions freely. This didn't displease me, as I had decided to continue to play the fool. When I got to the mosque on the rue Myrrha, I caught sight of Karim from afar, with Mehdi (whom I knew from the Palais de Justice) and a third man in Pakistani dress. I greeted them, starting with Mehdi and Karim, who introduced the third brother: 'Djamel, this is Abu Salsabyl.'

'*Asslam-o-Alaikum* [May peace be with you], my brother,' I said.

This brother replied in strangely accented Arabic. From his build and his accent, I deduced that he was a convert. Was he another of Karim's imitators? It's highly possible.

The pseudonym he had chosen for himself made me smile. It is a first name which was commonly used by the Arab tribes over fourteen centuries ago. Even a practising Muslim would not dare give his children a name like that. It's as if a French family gave their son the name Vercingetorix. This choice of name confirmed what I knew about the zeal which recent converts show in their practice of religion; they turn themselves into Muslims in the same way as people who join sects that preach strange behaviour. This convert also went by the name of Younès. I learned from Karim that his real first name was Thomas.

Karim was keen to introduce me to the restaurateur who financed the restaurant which served the free meals. He said goodbye to the two other brothers and asked me to follow him to the restauranteur's place near the mosque on the rue Myrrha. My intuition didn't mislead me: knowing the interest which Islamists show in social action, I was inclined to think that the 'generous benefactor' was a fundamentalist, and I was right.

I can recognize them easily, not from their beards but by their behaviour, their language and in their habits. The restaurateur, who was around forty, was somewhat reserved. He looked at me distrustfully. He explained that he acted charitably in this way 'for Allah'. Even when they kill, the fundamentalists do it 'for Allah'. He could equally well have used the same tone to justify any murder.

We made an appointment to film 'the positive work of the Muslims' and after a short discussion we left him. Karim had to go to the post office to send a money order to a brother in prison.

'Who is it for?'

'Smaïn Aït Ali Belkacem.'

I discovered that Karim was really close to the perpetrators

78

of the 1995 attacks and especially to Belkacem, the second of the two men found guilty in the trial. At the post office in Barbès, Karim told me about the trip he had to make to London with some brothers during the holidays at the end of the year.

'Do you want to come with us, Djamel?'

'What are you going to do over there?'

'We're going to meet some of the brothers. We have some work to do . . .'

'What sort of work?'

'I can't tell you anything just now. If you come with us, you'll see.'

'*Inshallah*, I shall come with you.'

Generally, when a terrorist talks about 'work', there is reason to worry. When they commit a terrorist act, they say they are 'working', likewise when they are preparing some sort of action, or when they have to do something illegal. Did Karim and some of the others have an attack to plan for in London? I don't know, but what I *am* sure of is that he and the other brothers often mentioned in my presence the arrest of Abu Qatada by Scotland Yard, one of the ideologues of international terrorism, who is close to Bin Laden. I often heard them say that the 'English could make trouble for themselves if they continue to persecute the brothers'. That said, it may very well be that these were nothing more than the words of a group of fanatics.

Naturally, if the brothers wanted to take me with them to London, I was not going to refuse; I had decided to see my investigation through to the end.

That day, all the brothers seemed to be looking at me in a

strange way and I didn't understand why. I had to wait until the end of my discussion with Karim to find out that I had shocked them a little. I was wearing a black beret to protect my head from the rain. Karim was looking at me in an awkward way, but I could see that he couldn't bring himself to tell me why. And so I asked him: 'What's the matter, Karim? I have the impression that you've been wanting to tell me something for a while . . .'

'It's your beret.'

'What's wrong with my beret?'

'Forgive me, brother, but in that beret, you look like an orthodox Jew. Our religion forbids us from looking like Jews or infidels.'

I didn't know whether to laugh or cry. I thought I had reached the heart of Muslim fundamentalism, but in fact perhaps what I had really reached was the heart of human stupidity. I pretended to feel outraged by the sentence which Karim had just imposed on me.

'I look like a Jew? Oh, that's terrible. I'm going to throw this piece of junk away right now,' I said, referring to the hat.

'No, don't throw it away! Sell it to an infidel and then you'll get some money to buy sweets for the children.'

I took off the beret and put it in my briefcase, almost apologizing to Karim, who puffed his chest out, doubtless believing that he had before him material which could be shaped to his will, like the young men he usually indoctrinated. After this 'very interesting' exchange I said goodbye to Karim. It was half past four and I took a taxi so as to be home with my family in time for the end of the fast. As soon as I was in the taxi, I moved my watch back to my right hand, put my wedding ring on – and my beret.

During the next three days my only contact with Karim was on the phone. I wanted to get some rest and to resume some sort of normal life. In the course of one of our brief telephone calls, I told Karim that I would come the following week with a camera to film all the 'charitable works' which he took part in. Besides the free restaurant, he had told me about his regular hospital visits. He went there with the brothers to bring the good news and comfort to the sick, especially those who were Muslim. Through this type of action, Islamists try to rally to their cause the most vulnerable members of society. In this way they hope to bring Muslims back to Islam and – why not? – to convert some non-Muslims. I was therefore keen to film these activities with the France 2 crew so as to show the ambivalence which characterizes the Islamists' approach.

Monday 25 November 2002

I had arranged to meet Karim at the mosque on the rue Myrrha at the time of the *Asr* prayers. I arrived a few minutes late and the prayers had already begun. When they were over, I looked around but Karim wasn't there. I found him on the first floor of the mosque, deep in conversation with a young man. I gestured to him to let him know that I would wait for him outside.

Almost as soon as I got outside, I saw two men coming towards me. It was a disaster – I knew one of them very well. He was Lyes Laribi, an Algerian Islamist and former FIS activist, one of those individuals who portray themselves in France as victims, and all the while the fundamentalist party for which they campaigned and continue to campaign remains accountable for tens of thousands of deaths in Algeria. With teeth bared and eyes glaring he came towards me. 'What are you doing here, you filthy dog?' he asked.

I shall never forget that moment or the way I managed to keep my cool. Karim could come out at any moment, and if he found me in the middle of a fight with an Islamic militant, I was done for. So I had little time to sort out the problem I had suddenly been faced with. I decided to risk everything.

'Are you talking to me, my brother?'

'Yes, I'm talking to you, you filthy dog.'

The man's anger redoubled, but my question and my nonchalance had, I felt, thrown him a little.

'Do you know me?'

'Of course I know you. You're Mohamed Sifaoui, the journalist.'

'You're mistaken, my brother.'

'Your name isn't Mohamed Sifaoui?'

'No, absolutely not. You're mistaken.'

Faced with the calm I was displaying, the other man took Lyes Laribi by the arm and said, 'It's not him. I told you it wasn't. He just looks like him.'

Lyes Laribi was confused.

'Excuse me, brother. I thought you were a filthy infidel, a journalist who's been insulting Muslims for years.'

'Next time you should be sure of who people are before you attack them in the street. What you just did isn't worthy of a good Muslim.'

'Forgive me again. But believe me, you look exactly like him. Without the beard you'd be his double. But he doesn't practise his faith as you do and doesn't go to the mosque. And what's more, he's a coward. He would never have dared come here. He knows that if the brothers catch him, he's dead.'

Our conversation had gone on long enough. Karim would be coming out of the mosque at any moment. I had already played with chance long enough. I took advantage of my phone ringing to say goodbye to Lyes Laribi, wishing him a good Ramadan with a smile. If Lyes Laribi happens to read this book, I would like to confirm that it was indeed me that he talked to on Monday 25 November 2002, on the rue Myrrha.

As I answered my phone, I headed towards an adjacent

street to escape the man who had recognized me. I made an excuse and hung up almost at once so that I would be able to walk more quickly. Finally I got to the boulevard Barbès. My telephone rang again and this time it was Karim.

'Where are you, Djamel?'

'I'm not far from the mosque. Let's meet on boulevard Barbès.'

It was vital that Lyes Laribi didn't see me with Karim. That would risk him asking questions about me. And if Karim introduced me as a journalist, I was done for. A double with the same background, age and profession would have been too much – even someone with limited intelligence would have realized the deception.

Karim joined me a few minutes later. We went for a walk around the area, but as I was still preoccupied by thoughts of Lyes Laribi, I claimed I had an urgent problem to sort out and took off. That day, Karim had wanted us to break the fast together and then wanted to take me to an exorcism. He had declared himself a healer and he told me that he sometimes recited verses from the Quran over Muslims suffering from psychological problems. Many credulous people still believe in these practices and put their trust in any charlatan who comes along. Knowing that these exorcisms can last several hours, I wasn't keen to attend. So I said goodbye to Karim and agreed to meet the following day. Since the beginning of my investigation, I had been very lucky, but the incident with Lyes Laribi had emphasized that my luck had its limits.

Tuesday 26 November 2002

Karim and I were due to meet at the mosque on rue Polonceau during the *Dohr* (middle of the day) prayers. When I got there at 1 p.m., Karim was already waiting for me. We prayed together and afterwards he gave me the keys to a safe house where he had been staying for several days on the rue Boissieu in the Barbès district.

'Here's a spare set of keys. When we leave the mosque, follow me and stay twenty metres or so behind to make sure that no one's following me. When I go into the building, wait five minutes before you come in. It's on the first floor on the left.'

I listened carefully to Karim's instructions and then reminded him that the team from France 2 were going to join me to complete the interview we had begun three weeks earlier.

'Do you really trust them, Djamel?'

'Absolutely. There's nothing to fear.'

'OK, but don't tell them it's a safe house. Tell them the apartment belongs to a friend who's gone away for a few days.'

'Don't be afraid, my brother, they won't even ask me questions.'

Reassured by my words, Karim agreed to the interview. He left the mosque first. I stayed behind as arranged and took the opportunity to call the France 2 team to let them know where we would be filming. Karim went along the boulevard de Rochechouart and at a particular point crossed the road. I followed. I stopped in front of a shop window to let him get ahead. That was when I noticed a man following him: he looked like a policeman. He was carrying a rucksack and walking with a certain casualness, but he never took his eyes off Karim. When he got to the rue Boissieu, I saw Karim open the door to the building, and take a quick look around as he did so. He glanced in my direction one last time before going into the building. The man with the rucksack was on the pavement opposite and had seen everything. I walked around the building and found myself back in front of the entrance five minutes later. I had lost sight of the man with the rucksack.

Karim opened the door.

'No one followed us?'

'I didn't see anything out of the ordinary,' I said, not mentioning the little game I had just witnessed.

The two-room apartment was completely run-down. In one room there was bedding piled up. The other room was tidier: a foam-rubber mattress on the floor, religious books and audio cassettes on the mantelpiece, a stool, a prayer mat, a chair, and a military uniform were all that the room contained. From the number of bags in the other room, several people had clearly passed through the apartment. Karim told me that several brothers went there when they feared a police raid on their homes. He proudly showed me an enormous bunch of keys to prove that he had several other safe houses, and asked me if I too had keys to empty apartments.

'It's very important, Djamel. It could be of use to brothers who are on the run or passing through Paris.'

My phone rang and interrupted this conversation: the France 2 team had arrived in the district. I had scarcely opened the door to the building, when I found myself face to face with the man with the rucksack. He was talking to someone on the phone. When he saw me, he turned round and looked the other way. I was therefore sure that the police had spotted me; they must have been convinced that I belonged to Karim's group. As I had nothing to feel guilty about, I decided to continue my investigation. If they'd arrested me, I would have explained everything to them. In any case, I want to emphasize that if I had had knowledge of a planned attack, I would have gone straight to the police station to alert the authorities. I want to make this clear in order to respond in advance to any questions about my attitude if I had found myself in such a situation. But we had not yet come to that point.

I quickly briefed my colleagues and checked my hidden camera, and then we went into the flat, where I rapidly made the introductions. The camera was set up, and the interview could begin. Karim wanted to talk about jihad. Once again, he reiterated his admiration for Osama Bin Laden and also admitted that sooner or later he would go to Chechnya to fight the Russians. We asked him a question about the risk of a terrorist attack on France. Karim tried to reassure us: he told us that there was no risk to France, and went as far as to compare Jacques Chirac to Negus of Abyssinia, who welcomed Muslims perse-

1. Members of the Quraych tribe, who lived in Mecca and whose leaders were opposed to the advent of Islam and the prophethood of Mohamed.

cuted by the Quraysh[1] during the Mahommedan era. It was impossible not to smile at this comparison. A few minutes later we had a break in the filming so that Karim could prepare coffee for his non-Muslim guests and I followed him into the kitchen.

'Were you serious when you claimed that Bin Laden didn't intend to strike France? Do you think he will or he won't?'

'Oh yes, of course he will. Do you think he is just fooling around? Shall I let you hear the latest recording by the sheikh [Osama Bin Laden] broadcast on Al Jazeera?'

'So that was all just put on for the camera just now? Now I can tell when you're telling the truth and when you're lying!'

He laughed. 'Ah good! You know when I am telling the truth and when I'm lying! You've worked me out, Djamel.' He laughed again.

'I'm your brother. That's why I've worked you out. I think like you.'

Karim was demonstrating once again his double-speak, an activity at which he excelled. What he actually believed was always the exact opposite of what he reserved for the infidels. The double-speak, *takiya* as the Islamists call it, is a technique to use in times of jihad 'with the enemy'. Never divulging your intentions or what you really think to a non-Muslim is the rule for all fundamentalists. That's how organizations or individuals which draw their doctrine from hard-core fundamentalism obligingly allow themselves to be labelled with the qualifier 'moderate' by naive Westerners who judge them exclusively by what they say. One of them denounces the attacks of 11 September, and is therefore a 'moderate', even if he is in favour of stoning women who commit adultery; another declares himself to be against the actions of Bin Laden and is thus also a 'moderate', even if he campaigns day and night for girls to wear the veil in state school. This Western naivety has often allowed fundamentalists to pass themselves off as respectable characters. The Afghan commander, Ahmed Shah Massoud, under whose aegis several international terrorists were trained, is without doubt the most salient example of this; his opposition to the Taliban has been enough to make him a hero.

After the interview, Karim suggested going to the free restaurant and naturally we went along. We wanted to film him at work, especially as a few days previously when I went with him to the restaurant Karim had tried to proselytize anyone who came in search of food and human company. Karim helped the people who ran the restaurant, but in particular looked after the place of prayer nearby. This place had been given to them by the council of the 18th *arrondissement*, who were certainly unaware that it permitted Islamists to extend their social action through proselytism.

At the end of the fast, Karim asked the other brothers to close the doors of the restaurant. 'Don't serve anything to eat before prayers,' he told one of the people in charge of the restaurant.

Karim led the prayers. Before he began, he asked all the faithful to make invocations for 'the victory of the brother mudjahidins'. In his every act, he made sure he mentioned the 'holy war'. I noticed that throughout the period I was in touch with him his whole life was centred on this question. At the end of the prayers, a man of around fifty began taking some photos. I asked Karim if he knew him.

'No, I don't know him, but I'm going to ask to see his papers.'

This was no sooner said than done. The man complied and took a card from his wallet. He was a member of the FNMF (the National Federation of French Muslims). I decided to ask him some questions.

'Why are you taking photos?'

'You know, my brother, we have regular meetings at the Ministry of the Interior. They're to show [Nicolas] Sarkozy [the French Interior Minister] that Muslims know how to do things right . . .'

This federation, which takes part in consultations initiated by the Ministry of the Interior with the aim of creating a representative authority of French Muslims, wanted to appropriate Karim and the other brothers' initiative.

Wednesday 27 November 2002

Day with Karim alone, who wanted to take me with him round the hospitals visiting the sick. His gentle side was to be on display on this occasion for the benefit of the France 2 film crew. Karim had himself suggested that they should be present so that they could film the 'good works of Muslims'. We had agreed to meet at the mosque on rue Polonceau. I arrived at the moment for the *Dohr* prayer. Karim was already there. As soon as the prayers were over, Karim suggested going to the market to buy some fruit for the sick. On the way, I pressed him gently. During our first filmed interview, Karim had revealed that it was 'problems with the Algerian authorities' which had forced him into exile. In the second interview, the day before, he claimed that he 'had never had problems with the Algerian authorities'. I wanted to confront him with this contradiction. At first he was astonished, but he ended up asking me to keep the second version and forget the first. He went on to talk about his French nationality, of which he was at risk of being stripped as had happened to Kamel Daoudi and Omar Saiki, two Islamists with links with international terrorism. This issue preoccupied him; he was afraid of being extradited to Algeria. I tried to reassure him.

After we had bought some fruit, Karim and I joined the France 2 crew, who were waiting for us near the boulevard Barbès. We were then going to go to the Lariboisière hospital, which was close by. Karim told us that he regularly made visits there.

When we arrived, a security man stopped us going in with our camera, though we had asked for permission to film. Karim appeared astonished by this decision. I played along in order to gain credibility in his eyes. I was especially rude to the security man, to whom I'd like to offer my sincere apologies. Karim looked at me with a smile, visibly delighted with how I had reacted. He allowed himself an ironic remark: 'Why don't they let us in? Do they think we are going to kill the patients? The French are completely mad . . .'

'Tell me, who should be killed?'

'Ah, if I come across [general] Khaled Nezzar[1] or [general] Lamari,[2] you'll see . . .'

'What will I see?'

'I swear, if I see them, you won't recognize me. Unless they kill me first . . .'

'I could come with you . . .'

'No, no, brother. Paradise is my goal. You know, killing people like them brings you closer to God.'

As he spoke these words, Karim was salivating. He was no longer a pious Muslim, ready to make himself useful to members

1. Khaled Nezzar is a former Algerian minister of defence who has now retired. He was in charge of the army when it decided to suspend the electoral process in Algeria, which is why Algerian Islamists detest him so intensely.
2. Mohamed Lamari is the chief of staff of the Algerian army. From 1992 he has been in charge of the anti-terrorist campaign.

of his community, the likeable brother who was forever smiling, or the man of integrity whose life was devoted to religion. His expression had hardened. It resembled that of a potential murderer, of a terrorist who 'loves death as we love life'.

After his extreme reaction, which revealed all the hatred he felt towards those in power in Algeria, Karim gave me a lesson in how the brothers prepare for an attack: 'When our brothers in Algeria want to get arms through a police checkpoint, they use two cars. In the first there'll be four men with beards who are not wanted by the police, and in the second, four young men who are clean-shaven. The car radio will be playing full blast, and they'll look like they don't have a care in the world. The police will stop the car with the bearded men and let the second car full of guns and explosives through . . .' He laughed.

'So they won't find anything on us now!' He laughed again.

'When we're asked to shave our beards off, then you'll see . . .' and he laughed a third time.

While we'd been having this discussion at the hospital entrance, the France 2 crew were trying to negotiate permission to film. The next moment, Karim happened to recognize another bearded man.

'*Asslam-o-Alaikum* [Peace be upon you], brother. How are you? Can I introduce our brother, Djamel?'

Karim introduced me to Ahmed Ouerghemi, a Tunisian fundamentalist and political asylum seeker, who has lived in France for seventeen years. He confided to me that he had been slogging away for several years without managing to get his papers. I quickly realized that he knew Karim very well and that he also attended the Omar mosque in Belleville. This remarkable individual has sent death threats and insults quite openly by fax and mail to the Tunisian president, Zine el Abidine Ben Ali, whose administration refuses to give his wife and children passports. He asserted proudly to me that his only views on nationality could be summed up in the following words: 'There is no God but God and Mohamed is his prophet.' Islamists consider themselves to belong to an Oumma[1] in which the principle of nationality has no place.

When the France 2 crew returned, they confirmed that we hadn't been granted permission to film inside the hospital. I introduced Ouerghemi to my colleagues. He completely changed his tune and declared that he was 'against terrorism and against all forms of violence', but scarcely had the TV journalists turned their backs when he said to me with a smile, 'You must never show those people [non-Muslims] that you belong to the jihad.' I was once again in the midst of double-speak.

Ahmed Ouerghemi went on to claim that he had already worked with members of the GIA between 1992 and 1994 before his arrest by the French police. 'I was going to join the Algerian resistance when I was arrested in France,' he explained. He concluded with the words, 'Djamel, my brother, you must constantly wage jihad until the banner of Islam is raised as high as it can possibly be.'

I asked him how he managed to live without a job or any

1. *Oumma*: the 'Islamic nation', which will rally the whole Muslim world under a single banner.

other means. 'I deal in false documents. I sell forged passports to brothers who are wanted by the police.'

'That's lucky,' I said. 'I'm often in touch with brothers who are looking for false documents.'

'That's no problem, Djamel, I'll give you my phone number. In three days I can get you a top quality fake passport. I get them from a town hall where I've got friends.'

I took his telephone number and said goodbye to my new brother, promising to call him very soon.

Karim was disappointed that the hospital management had refused us entry. He hadn't been following the conversation I had had with Ahmed. The hospital director had agreed to allow the TV crew in to explain the reasons for her refusal: we didn't belong to any known organization and therefore it was natural that she should refuse us access to the sick. I can report on the evidence of a later occasion that without the presence of the cameras, it is possible for Islamists to visit Muslim patients, especially if the patients have no objection.

We parted at 5 p.m. Karim had been invited to dinner by the family of an Islamist prisoner whose name he didn't tell me.

THE NETWORK ABROAD

Friday 29 November 2002

I was meeting Karim at 3 p.m. at the Couronnes metro station in Belleville, near the Abu-Bakr mosque. The day before I had arranged to see him along with some other brothers who, according to him, wanted to meet me. That morning I went to the offices of France 2 to prepare for the meeting. Karim had told me that he would be 'with someone whose name has become known through the press'. He didn't want to say more on the phone. Who was this 'someone'? The question was nagging away at me. Who could it be? Omar Saiki? Someone who knew me? That was my main fear – finding myself face to face with an Islamist who recognized me. Before each meeting I felt stressed, but on this occasion I was really worried. My anxiety had increased since the incident with Lyes Laribi outside the mosque on the rue Myrrha. Nonetheless I tried to stay in control and keep my cool. I constructed disaster scenarios in my head and imagined how I would deal with them.

After I had made my preparations and set up my hidden camera as usual, the France 2 crew and I went to our meeting. We arrived in Belleville at exactly 3 p.m. Karim was waiting for us. He was indeed with another brother, a smiling man of about forty, who wore a thick beard and glasses which gave him an intelligent look. I was reassured in part by this brother's smile and his warm handshake. I didn't recognize his face. Did he recognize me? Evidently not.

Karim made the introductions very quickly: this new brother was called Khamis Ali Majeri. He was a Tunisian imam at the mosque on the rue Myrrha. Straight away he mentioned his 'problems' with the police and certain sections of the media, especially *Le Parisien*, which according to him had libelled him. With the France 2 team there, he replied to my questions very guardedly; our brother clearly didn't like the cameras. When we wanted to move on to questions about terrorism and the attacks of 11 September, Khamis resorted to evasion. He told me privately that he didn't want to talk about that sort of subject with non-Muslims. Khamis belongs to a dissident branch of Nahda, the Tunisian Islamist party run by the highly controversial Rached Ghanouchi, who is currently taking refuge in London. He said he was also close to Kerkar, another figure in Tunisian Islamism, who sought asylum in France and is currently under house arrest in Digne-les-Bains.

The French police interviewed Khamis over a sermon he disseminated in which he gave some sort of legitimacy to terrorism by linking it to the Muslim religion. He doesn't hesitate, moreover, to state loudly and clearly that 'terrorism is a sacred term in Islam'. As far as I'm concerned, people like him are as dangerous as those who plant the bombs. It is people like him who, through their wrong interpretations of the sacred text, manipulate the minds of the young with the sole aim of sending them to their deaths and thereby causing the deaths of innocent people. After a short discussion with Khamis, I agreed that I would get in touch with him again after Ramadan.

In the course of that day we filmed as planned some sequences with Karim in bookshops which sell Islamist literature. When I rejoined the France 2 crew I noticed the presence of another bearded man, a Tunisian called Mourad who knew Karim. The two men were talking privately, looking in my direction; I was probably the subject of their conversation. I kept a good distance from them so as not to disturb them.

In the bookshop I browsed among the various works on offer. They had everything from Ibn Taimiya to Al-Qaradawi, via the Otheimine and Ibn Al-Baz, the brothers Hani and Tarek Ramadan, and other ideologues of the Islamist movement. Enough to fill the heads of three generations of Muslims and non-Muslims alike. Everything available was affordable since Islamist literature, especially the Wahabi stuff, is sold at unbeatable prices because they are subsidized by Saudi organizations responsible for spreading the Wahabi doctrine to the four corners of the earth. Among the books an 'original work' clearing Bin Laden of blame for the 11 September attacks was prominently displayed. Karim said with irritation, 'That sort of book tries to show that we are not capable of preparing that type of operation. We say to its author that we *are* capable of that – and of worse than that!'

By around half past four we had finished in the bookshop and we suggested to Karim and the other brothers that we went to eat together after the end of the fast at 5 p.m. We invited our 'friends' to a restaurant run by an Algerian Islamist Karim had introduced me to who is close to the FIS. Karim accepted our invitation without hesitation. It was during this meal that things would turn really serious. Karim introduced Mourad to me at greater length and told him in front of me that I wanted to meet Omar Saiki. The Tunisian looked at me and smiled, then said, 'I'll call him and ask him to meet you, *Inshallah*, but first we must have a talk together . . .'

I had definitely had a stroke of luck. Mourad explained that he had been watching me continually and that he could see in me a 'sincere brother' and a defender of the cause of Islam.

'Continue like that because what you are doing is also jihad.'

These words resembled Karim's of a few weeks before when he asked me if I could 'help the cause by showing the actions of Al Qaeda in a positive light'. As far as they were concerned, I was a propagandist for the Islamist movement.

During the meal, Mourad continued to give me the low-down. He told me that he had come specially to meet me at Saiki's request. He had to assure himself that the description which Karim had given of me wasn't wrong. Karim's role in the network was limited to recruiting new followers and introducing them to different 'brothers' so that they could all give their opinions, and then sending them to London, where all the 'brains' of international Islamism are based.

In this way I could retrace the path of young men like Djamel

Loiseau, who was first indoctrinated in Belleville, and then began to go to the Pakistani-run Ali mosque in Paris's Faubourg Saint-Denis, before being sent to the London mosques, which were the last stop before landing at the Pakistan–Afghan border in the heart of Osama Bin Laden's foreign legion or else in the Caucasus among the 'Chechen Arabs'. Evidently the network I was in contact with was one link among many in the Islamist network.

Mourad was convinced that I belonged to the Islamist movement, not only in my politics but also from the point of view of dogma and ideology. I had, it is true, put forward arguments dear to the hearts of fundamentalists. I also quoted to him the words of Ibn Taimiya and contemporary Wahabi theologians about jihad.

At the end of the meal, Mourad told me that he was going to ring Saiki to organize a meeting. He carefully noted down my name and telephone number in a small diary. Two hours later, as I was about to catch the metro, he called to arrange to see me the next day near the mosque.

'I've got news for you,' he told me, without mentioning Saiki's name.

Saturday 30 November 2002

At around 11 a.m. I left the France 2 offices carrying my hidden camera as usual. At precisely midday, the taxi set me down at rue Jean-Pierre-Timbaud a few metres from the mosque. Mourad wasn't there. I waited patiently, looking at the hawkers and illegal street traders who were particularly busy during the month of Ramadan.

My mind wandered back through the events I had experienced during the past few weeks. I found myself thinking over all the details. I had to collect my thoughts so as to be consistent in what I said and to avoid lapsing into over-familiarity in my meetings with the brothers, which had become routine. I had taken on a new personality: Djamel Mostaghanemi had nothing to do with Mohamed Sifaoui. I had gained a better understanding of the intellectual and moral disaster experienced by those who fall into the net of religious fundamentalism. When I was with my 'brothers' I became like them, and sometimes worse than them. Without going too far, I tried every day by subtle means to show them that I was in complete agreement with their deadly views. The exercise was dangerous, but above all it was tiring. I would like to emphasize that this exercise showed me how draining hypocrisy can be. In the end, there is no substitute for naturalness, honesty and spontaneity.

By half past twelve, Mourad still hadn't shown up for our meeting. As I didn't have his number, I couldn't phone him. I took it in my stride and went towards the Omar mosque, where Mehdi, Sofiane, Karim and some other brothers were on a 'spiritual retreat' during the last ten days of Ramadan, when they devoted themselves to prayer and invocation. These retreats allow them to meet together and to discuss different topical questions: questions of religion, politics or dogma, but also possible action they could engage in at every level.

They were ensconced in a corner in the basement of this mosque run by Tunisian extremists. Imam Hammami, a Tunisian who had just served a four-year sentence in his own country had recently come back here. I fail to understand how an imam who has been in trouble with the authorities in his own country for his Islamist activities is still allowed to hold sway in France without any problem.

I found my brothers deep in meditation but they were clearly happy to see me. I asked Karim whether he had run into Mourad. He said he hadn't, but he talked about my imminent meeting with Omar Saiki and confirmed that Saiki was in London. 'He's with Abu Hamza,' he said, adding, 'I'll arrange for you to stay at Finsbury Park.'

I explained that I'd rather go to a hotel because the France 2 crew would be with me. It would have been dangerous for me to spend a night in the Finsbury Park mosque; I risked coming face to face with Algerian Islamists who knew me. In addition, Abu Hamza's group are far more hard-line than the Islamists active in France. The imam of the Finsbury Park mosque is an old campaigner. This one-eyed man with an amputated hand is a veteran of the first Afghan war.

At 1.20 p.m. the muezzin announced the *Dohr* (middle of the day) prayer. Mourad still hadn't come. Having recited the prayer with Karim and the other 'brothers', I decided to head back to the Couronnes metro station in the hope of finding Mourad. At all events, I had no intention of leaving the neighbourhood before I had seen him. As I left the mosque, I switched off my hidden camera. That was unfortunate, as a few seconds later Mourad came down the rue Jean-Pierre-Timbaud heading in my direction. When he saw me he looked pleased. He was clearly happy to have found me. We exchanged *salams* [greetings]. He apologized for being late and explained that he hadn't even had time to pray. He went straight on to the subject which interested us, Omar Saiki. As I hadn't had time to switch my camera back on, I interrupted him and suggested that we went to the mosque first.

I made use of the time while he was praying to switch my camera on. A few minutes later, Mourad came and leaned on the wall beside me at the back of the prayer room. 'We're going to London together next Saturday after *Eid* [the festival which ends Ramadan],' he said. I remembered that he had told me the day before that he had a Tunisian passport and consequently would need to get a visa.

'Do you think you'll have your visa in time?' I asked innocently.

'I'll use a false French passport,' was his straightforward reply. I told him I thought that could be risky.

'No risk. I'm used to it,' he said with assurance. He added, 'Don't worry. We won't have any problem.'

Having settled that question, we launched into a long discussion, a vast survey of the Islamist movement throughout the world. We talked about Islam in Tunisia, Algeria, France, Morocco, Afghanistan, Pakistan, and other places besides. Mourad was keen to justify the actions of the young Frenchmen who followed the path of jihad. In particular he spoke about two of his former disciples, Djamel Loiseau and Brahim Yadel, who is being held at Guantanamo Bay. As Karim had done a few days before, he explained that his role was to incite young people to go and join the jihad against powers such as the USA and Israel. He told me too that he had never been arrested, 'just called by the DST [anti-terrorist branch] for an interview'.

'After they'd questioned me, all they said was that I was a good Muslim,' he added.

He was very proud of this assessment supposedly made by the French anti-terrorist police. Mourad readily presents himself as a pacifist who wouldn't hurt a fly. To his way of thinking, he is not doing anything serious in offering religious training to young people to turn them into fanatics and human bombs.

After the mid-afternoon prayer (*Al Asr*) we joined the other brothers again. Karim wanted to introduce me to an Algerian, Ahmed Kheïreddine. I quickly learned that he had been arrested on suspicion of financing terrorist cells through his activities linked to smuggling and counterfeiting. He had also been indirectly linked to the 'Roubaix gang', a name which had been on everyone's lips in 1996, and also to the 'Bosnian fighters' for whom, by his own admission, he obtained false documents. He told me that he was pending trial. I spent a further three-quarters of an hour with the group so as to hear as much as possible from this newcomer.

When I had learned as much as I could from him, at least for an initial meeting, I gave him my phone number and said goodbye. I wanted to leave. My hidden camera was heating up and was making me enormously uncomfortable since, as a result of being obliged to stay on the floor in the prayer room, it had shifted and was now making a strange bump under my trousers below my zip. Now I was really embarrassed. I had to get up, but, so as not to take undue risks, I decided to button up my raincoat in spite of the suffocating heat in the basement. The heat only increased my feeling of unease. I felt dizzy and extremely uncomfortable and had a terrible headache. Mehdi, Sofiane, Karim and the others went on talking to me but I couldn't understand anything. I could no longer hear. The hidden camera was now visible under my trousers; it formed an enormous bump which threatened to give me away. I foresaw disaster. I thought about my wife and children, my family and friends, and also about the thousands of victims killed by Islamist terrorism: the people decapitated in Algeria, the victims of the Paris attacks, and those of 11 September. I cursed the recklessness which had pushed me to pursue such an idiotic career and this mad investigation.

Suddenly Mehdi cracked a joke, and held out his huge giant's hand. I found myself bursting out laughing, but I was only laughing because the others were laughing, without knowing why. A joke from the lips of an Islamist had saved my investigation and probably my life. I created a diversion saying, 'Let's cut out the jokes. We shouldn't forget our prayers and invocations. We're in a mosque, remember.'

As I spoke I stood up, taking care to conceal my camera, which slid down my right leg. This subterfuge was like a breath of air to a dying man. Having shaken them by the hand, I headed towards the door with Mourad and Ahmed Kheïreddine. I went straight to the toilet, not to relieve a call of nature but to put the hidden camera back in its place. I was safe at last, at least for the time being.

Perhaps, having given me a warning, chance had granted me a reprieve.

We were now in the last week of Ramadan. Karim had one major preoccupation – collecting the *zakat* for *Eid*.[1] Usually, he told me, this collection was made by the Omar mosque. But this year, according to what he said, he had agreed with imam Hammami that he would be paid a percentage of the *zakat* collected by the mosque. Karim must have told the imam that this money would go to fund Islamist prisoners, as the imam accepted with some reluctance, according to Karim. He also told me that in order to collect the maximum amount of money, he was planning on also making a collection himself on the day of *Eid* outside the Daawa mosque on the rue de Tanger in the 19th *arrondissement*.

1. *Zakat* for *Eid* or *zakat El Fitr*: obligatory charitable donation which every Muslim has to make at the end of Ramadan. The amount is fixed every year by the religious authorities. In 2002 it was raised to 5 Euros per person.

I wanted to get a better understanding of his relationship with imam Hammami, so decided to press Karim: 'Are you sure he'll keep his word?'

'It's in his interest. He doesn't know what I'm capable of . . .'

'What could you do if he decided not to give you a percentage of the *zakat* collection?'

'Wait and see . . .'

Karim suddenly became menacing. He showed his real nature each time an event or even a simple suggestion threatened to thwart him. His smile was then replaced by a serious and menacing expression. Clearly the fact that he was not in control of the situation in the mosque exasperated him. I could see that there was an invisible arm-wrestling match going on between Karim and the other brothers on one side and imam Hammami and his circle on the other. This wrestling match was perfectly illustrated during these final days of Ramadan. In fact, those who were officially in charge upstairs at the mosque used 'moderate' language, while Karim and the other brothers who occupied the basement during their spiritual retreat spoke about politics and jihad in radical and frankly war-mongering terms, which included threats towards the French state. The strange thing was that imam Hammami said nothing. It was obvious that he was unhappy, but still he stayed silent. He displayed a sort of fear of the inhabitants of his basement. I was told that he had gone down to see them to ask them to be careful about what they were saying: 'The mosque is under police surveillance. Do you want me to be put in prison?'

The following days I went to see the brothers every afternoon at the Omar mosque. I stayed three or four hours in order to gauge what was going on and to glean new information. In particular, I was getting ready for my trip to London, which was planned for the following Saturday, though with the Islamists nothing was ever certain. They were past masters at the art of completely changing their plans.

Each day Mourad would confirm to me when we were going. He was absolutely determined to come with me, and I couldn't understand why he would be prepared to run such a risk travelling with a false passport, just to take me to see Omar Saiki. The whole business was beginning to intrigue me.

Wednesday 4 December 2002

Eid was to be held on 5 or 6 December; on Wednesday we would find out which it was to be. I decided to spend the day with my brothers at the mosque. Karim was determined to go and make his collection outside the mosque on the rue de Tanger on the day of *Eid*. He had asked Mehdi to go along with him and I told them that I wanted to come too with the France 2 film crew. The two brothers made no objection.

To prepare for the day Karim decided to go and buy a *kamis*[1] for Mehdi, 'so that you look like a good Muslim' as he put it. Mehdi, it's worth reiterating, was completely under Karim's authority. Despite being 1.95m and weighing 142kg, this giant who had converted to Islam stayed completely in the background when Karim was there. The relationship between the two brothers was almost like a caricature: Mehdi, big and brawny, was submissive to the charisma of the small and stocky Karim. Karim held the trump cards which Mehdi lacked: he knew the Islamist ideology and dogma better than his convert, and Mehdi suffered from a sort of inferiority complex on account of this handicap. He tried to overcome this complex by asserting himself through his physical strength, which would, he claimed, enable him to 'kill infidels with [his] bare hands'.

1. *Kamis*: a long shirt worn by Islamists. The garment originates in the Gulf states and Saudi Arabia.

At the end of the day, we heard that *Eid* was to take place the following day. All the brothers therefore left their spiritual retreat in order to prepare themselves. Karim busied himself calling everyone he knew to ask them to bring him their *zakat* as soon as possible. I went home to spend the evening with my family, having arranged to meet Karim at 5 a.m. the following day, the hour of the morning prayer (*Sobh*). We were to meet at the Omar mosque and then go on to the rue de Tanger.

Thursday 5 December 2002

It was a holiday in the Muslim community, but an ordinary day for me. For almost three months I had completely neglected my family life. *Eid* is for Muslims what Christmas is for Christians and Yom Kippur is for Jews. Usually I spend the day with my wife and children, but this year I was obliged to break this rule. My days obeyed the rhythm of my brothers' days. I still had a few weeks to spend in their mad world. So on the morning of *Eid* I had to leave my private feelings to one side.

I had decided to impress my brothers, who had never seen me in the traditional dress, which is highly appreciated by fundamentalists. I chose an Afghan costume, a garment which I had bought in a market in Peshawar as a souvenir of my trip to Pakistan and Afghanistan. With my beard, which had now grown thick and my clothes, people looked at me worriedly that morning.

I was right: when Karim saw how I was dressed he looked very pleased. He said he was 'very proud' of me and even asked me to dress like that more often. To tell the truth, he wasn't happy seeing me dressed in jeans, pullover and parka. He wanted me to 'mark my difference', though he did show indulgence: 'Since you work, you can't always wear Muslim dress.'

Karim loved me to tell him about my trips to Pakistan. According to him, that was where you met 'true Muslims and mudjahidins'. He had never been there but someone talking to him about it allowed him to imagine travelling in a world he admired. He often asked me questions about the Pakistani Islamists and the 'fighters' I had met over there. I had no trouble answering his questions as I was very familiar with those circles. I had passed myself off as a 'brother' there and could quote the names of the Quranic schools I had visited and the Islamist leaders I had met. This personal history gave me additional credibility.

Immediately after the *Sobh* prayer at the Omar mosque, we went straight to the rue de Tanger, where Karim and Mehdi were going to begin their collecting work. Neither the driving rain nor the cold put them off. When they got near the Daawa mosque, the two brothers took up their position on the pavement, a box in their hands with 'zakat = 5 Euros' written on it. The faithful didn't wait to be asked: Karim and Mehdi had scarcely got into their places and already several people had slipped either coins or notes into both their boxes. It was a clear demonstration of the naivety of honest Muslims. The faithful didn't know that the two brothers were financing terrorists and perhaps even terrorism. That is why the collection in the future ought to be scrupulously regulated and rigorously controlled, by the authorities in the first place, but also by the Muslim community itself.

After collecting for an hour and a half, Mehdi came to see me and handed me a plastic bag full of notes and coins. He asked me to hide it in the car, which confirmed the extent of the confidence which my brothers now had in me. I called my colleagues from France 2 and asked them to come and film me counting the money in the car, which we did discreetly. The result: 1,000 Euros collected by Mehdi alone in under two hours. I learned later that the collection had brought the two brothers a little over 3,000 Euros in less than three hours. After the *Eid* prayer, Karim, Mehdi and I went to have an *Eid* breakfast in Barbès. On the way, Mehdi received a call on his mobile. He went off to take it while I was discussing with Karim how the money would be shared out. He told me that it would be divided into three parts: 'One share for the prisoners, one for Mehdi and me, and the third for the cause.'

Whoever collected the money, according to Karim, had the right to benefit from it. He didn't clarify, however, who would benefit from the money destined for 'the cause'. This third share would go to finance the purchase of arms, ammunition and everything required for the jihad. I discovered later that he sent some of the money collected in France to a contact abroad, but I never found out where exactly he was.

Mehdi was still on the phone. I was intrigued. Usually he spoke loudly, but now he was whispering. Eventually he completed his call, looked at Karim, and said in a low voice, 'It was Ammar.'

'Which Ammar?'

'Ammar! Our brother from the GSPC. He's asking if we can go to see him.'

I walked on, pretending not to have seen or heard any of this. The two brothers immediately changed the subject. A few minutes later they said they would have to go and meet some of their family. They still didn't want to involve me in 'sensitive' subjects, which was unsurprising since I hadn't yet proved myself.

When we got to the café, Karim took from his pocket a bundle of letters sent by brothers in prison thanking him for his generosity. He was unsparing in his praise for them: 'Between someone in poverty and a fighter, I'd always choose to help a fighter,' he liked to keep repeating. I got up to pay for our drinks, but Karim stopped me. 'I'll pay with the money from the collection. It's my right,' he said, taking a 20 Euro note out of the plastic bag, to the astonishment of the café owner, who had followed the whole performance.

It was time to part. My brothers had, I could tell, run into some unforeseen problem. I made myself scarce so as not to give the impression that I was too curious. We agreed to meet the next day in Belleville. I had to go there in any case to meet Mourad to work out the details of our visit to London.

Friday 6 December 2002

The second day of *Eid*. In Belleville the shops were open again
after the first day of the holiday. This district has been dominated
by the Islamists for several years; that is noticeable on occasions
such as this. Karim and the other brothers refer to areas like this
ironically as 'the liberated territories' or else 'the Islamic states'.
They have managed in a way to establish 'mini Islamic republics'
in the heart of the secular state.

I had only just arrived when some men I didn't know rushed
up to wish me a good *Eid*; I had become one of the regulars. All
the brothers now greeted me in the street. I couldn't help thinking about what a long way I had travelled in three months at the
heart of the Islamist movement.

At around 2 p.m. I came across Mourad and his cousin
Mohamed on the rue Jean-Pierre-Timbaud. We wished each
other a happy *Eid* and were about to go to the café when we saw
Karim with another man I didn't know. This newcomer stayed
with us for a few seconds before going off. He didn't want to disturb us. He knew that we were going to talk about our trip to
London. Islamist activists have a certain sense of propriety;
they don't get involved in what doesn't directly concern them.
Their relations are encrypted, coded. In our case, the link
between Saiki and me was Mourad, so Karim didn't get
involved with it. Mourad's cousin Mohamed also left us so that
we could talk privately. This way of behaving enables the

Islamists to minimize leaks and guarantee a certain discretion for their activities.

It was only when we were alone that Mourad brought up the subject of our trip to London. As I was half-expecting, everything that we had agreed seemed up in the air. In fact, it was worse than that: the trip was off.

'Why?' I asked, astonished by this sudden turnaround.

'I don't know. Imad[1] called me last night to tell me that he had changed his mind.'

'You can't be serious, Mourad. Call him back and tell him that I'll be in London in any case this weekend.'

After our coffee, Mourad asked me to go with him to a phone box. 'Let's call Imad.' This wasn't a bad idea: this phone call would let me have my first contact with the person I wanted to meet.

While Mourad was dialling, I made a point of memorizing the number: 00 44 79 40 79 . . . I quickly copied it down on a scrap of paper without Mourad noticing. The number he dialled did indeed belong to a mobile phone in the United Kingdom. Mourad started speaking, telling Imad about my surprise at the trip being called off. After a few minutes, Mourad asked me to speak to him. I took the receiver and began my 'speech'. Imad responded coldly at first – he seemed very distrustful indeed. He confirmed that he had agreed to meet me initially 'only because the brothers in Paris vouched for you'. Now that I had him at the end of the line, I wasn't going to let him get away without

1. Imad is Omar Saiki's pseudonym.

securing a meeting with him. Saiki ended up giving in, but stipulated that he would not tolerate the presence of cameras, or of women, or any non-Muslim journalists. I told him that I was working with a film crew who had to come to London for other reasons and it would be inappropriate to make them wait somewhere else during our meeting. 'There's a risk they'll ask questions,' I said challengingly, adding, 'Show them, brother, that we have nothing to hide.'

Evidently he was won round by my arguments, because Saiki agreed to the presence of my colleagues on condition that none of them spoke to him. The fact that he had been stripped of his French citizenship had made him very negative, indeed downright hostile, towards everything French. What he said to me on the phone revealed to me the degree of loathing he now felt towards France.

Before hanging up, I gave him my phone number so that we could have direct contact without having to go through Mourad if the worst came to the worst. As far as he was concerned, Saiki made clear that he wanted Mourad present at our meeting. That was awkward: Mourad could very well realize that my name wasn't Djamel Mostaghanemi when we went through passport controls. However, I didn't have any choice; I had to put myself through this new test of my nerves.

'I'll see you on Sunday,' Saiki added, claiming that something unexpected ruled a Saturday meeting out.

After my conversation with Saiki, I tried one last time to dissuade Mourad from coming with me.

'Are you coming with me?'

'Yes. As you heard, Imad absolutely insists that I'm there.'

'Aren't you afraid to travel with a false passport?'

'Don't worry, Djamel, that's my problem. I'm used to it . . .'

Mourad showed unfailing confidence. He wanted to come along and in any case, I told myself, if he got himself arrested, that was his problem. We parted, having agreed a time to meet on Sunday.

Saturday 7 December 2002

In the middle of the afternoon, I decided to take a walk round Belleville. I couldn't stop thinking about my journey the following day. My main fear was meeting Saiki with Islamists who might recognize me. I had decided to meet him in the city centre rather than near the London mosques; that way, if something went wrong, I would have much greater room for manoeuvre. Hamza is always surrounded by ruthless minders. There could be no question of my wandering around the London mosques with a hidden camera; body searches had become a regular thing since Islamist premises were infiltrated by BBC journalists.

I met Karim in Ménilmontant. Curiously, although he knew that I was due to meet the head of the network which had been dismantled in 1998, he didn't ask me any questions. He mainly wanted to hear my opinion of a cassette he had given me the day before. It was a recording of sermons by mudjahidin Arabs in Afghanistan – the usual fundamentalist propaganda about jihad, death, paradise and so on. This was how we got onto the subject of possible terrorist attacks in European countries.

'It's time for us to take action,' Karim told me.

'Take action? But are we supposed to do that?'

'Of course! The sheikh [Osama Bin Laden] has given the order.'

'What? Are you in touch with Bin Laden?'

He laughed. 'No, I'm not in touch with him, but in the last recording of his which appeared on Al Jazeera, he asked us to take action.'

And Karim began to explain, in fact to decode the latest message from Osama Bin Laden. According to him, besides enabling him to 'claim responsibility for attacks or show that he is still alive' these recordings also serve the function of 'sending messages to cells which identify with Al Qaeda's struggle'. So, if you believe Karim Bourti, Osama Bin Laden in his last recording asked different terrorist cells active in Europe and America to take action in the countries he mentioned: Canada, France, Germany, Great Britain and Italy. This information made me feel dizzy. Karim was apparently deciphering for me a semi-coded message from Osama Bin Laden. He didn't stop there but supported his claim by citing concrete examples: 'Haven't you heard about all the attacks which have been foiled since this message? In England, Italy and other places, attacks have been prepared, but Allah did not want them to take place.'

Karim, with a mocking smile, told me by way of conclusion, 'Don't worry, Djamel, it won't do any harm to wait.' For my brother, there was no doubt: 'France will sooner or later be the target of an attack.'

Through his words, Karim wanted to put pressure on me and push me to take active part in whatever act might be in preparation. He had asked me several times if I could gain access to sensitive sites with my press card. When I told him I could, he showed keen satisfaction and said, 'That's good.' He even went as far as to suggest that I got him blank press cards so that the brothers could make forgeries. This interest in cards brought to mind the assassination of General Mourad, the Afghan war leader. He was the victim of men claiming to be journalists, who booby-trapped their camera and caused it to explode when they were in front of him. Each day brought its new crop of information on the real mission of Karim and the brothers. If they weren't for the moment 'operationals' in the true sense of the word, they fulfilled an important logistical role. I was certain that if there were an attack aimed at France, one way or another some of them would have a hand in it.

After two hours with Karim, I went home. Before I went up to my flat, I stopped at a café to have a drink with a friend and relax a bit. Very few of my friends knew what I was doing. I had, though, told a few close friends and colleagues. The friend I was meeting did know, and our conversation allowed me to get things off my chest, and relieve some of the burden that weighed on my shoulders. It also let me get an outside perspective on the situation I was in. Spending three months with Islamists is without doubt a testing exercise for the nerves. I found myself in the company of criminals who didn't hesitate to applaud in my presence the murder of Algerian colleagues or other activists in political parties. Sometimes they even mentioned the names of victims of Islamist terrorism whom I knew personally, which always left me in an extremely distressed state. I too had to approve the deaths of those 'infidel allies of tyranny'.

While I was telling my friend how I felt, my phone rang. I answered, taking care to move away from the music which filled the café on that Saturday evening. This was a necessary precaution as Islamists are opposed to going to cafés which serve alcohol and play music. This was the right decision as it was Saiki. He was calling to say that he wouldn't be alone at the meeting, and that his decision was final as far as an interview on camera was concerned. He told me that Qamreddine Kherbane and Abdellah Anès alias Boudjemaa Bounouna would be with him – two of the big shots. Saiki was bringing me on a plate some of the most famous activists to whom I had devoted large sections of my previous book.[1] This was an ironic twist of fate: I was going to come face to face with two terrorists whose careers I knew back to front. It was an exceptional opportunity . . .

Qamreddine Kherbane is a former Algerian Air Force fighter pilot who left the forces to join the international Islamist movement. He went to Afghanistan in the 1980s to take part in the 'jihad against the Soviet army' and there he met all the leaders of international Islamist terror. He would go on to be one of the founders of the armed groups in Algeria before settling in France in the early 1990s.

Abdellah Anès is also an Afghan veteran. He was one of the closest collaborators of Abdellah Azzem, the Palestinian Islamist who directed Makteb El Khadamat, the recruiting office in Peshawar for Arab mudjahidins. Anès succeeded in winning the confidence of Azzem to the extent that he married Azzem's daughter and became his second in command. At this time,

---

1. *La France malade de l'islamisme: Menaces terroristes sur l'Hexagone* (le cherche midi, 2002).

Abdellah Anès was far more important in the hierarchy of Islamic fundamentalism than Osama Bin Laden. He got to know Kherbane somewhere between Pakistan and Afghanistan and in conjunction with him and other terrorists formed the first armed groups in Algeria. Like Kherbane, Anès went into exile in France after elections were suspended in Algeria and spent his time mainly on Islamist propaganda and the financing of the Algerian resistance. Kherbane and Anès were expelled by the French authorities in 1992 and sent to Pakistan. The two men now belong to the network of Afghan veterans.

So the next day I would reach a new stage. The meeting I had arranged wasn't with small fry but with big fish. Nothing to do with Karim, Mehdi, and their crew. This was a new level . . .

Sunday 8 December 2002

We'd planned to take the 8 a.m. train. Mourad and I had arranged to meet at around 7.30 at the gare du Nord, where we would be joined by the France 2 crew. By seven I was already having a coffee in a café opposite the station entrance. I had had a disturbed night – I hadn't been able to stop thinking about what awaited me this Sunday.

By 7.30 the France 2 crew had turned up but there was no sign of Mourad, so I decided to call his cousin, Mohamed. He told me that Mourad was just getting ready to leave. In the end we missed the train and caught the next one at nine.

To avoid anyone I met in London recognizing me, I dressed so that I didn't look like Mohamed Sifaoui normally did. I wore a black track suit with the hood up, and a hat. My beard and this get-up made me look like a petty criminal at the very least. Mourad was wearing Saudi dress. And so it was natural that we attracted the attention of the border police. It was clear that we were subjected to a spot check because of our race. Our passports were carefully examined before we got them back. If Mourad's passport was forged as he claimed, the police didn't notice anything. After the passport check I asked him about it. 'No, Djamel, it's genuine, don't worry,' he said casually. I realized then that he had in fact been testing me to make sure that I wasn't a mole: if I had alerted the police and the passport was genuine, he could immediately have concluded that I had betrayed him. This further detail encouraged the brothers to trust me even more. They subjected me to tests of this sort from time to time to reassure themselves as to my true motives.

On the Eurostar Mourad described his indignation at the sort of check we had just undergone: 'They're the ones who push people to commit attacks by suspecting all Muslims like that.' All through the journey we talked about religion and the 'issues which lay ahead for Muslims'. Mourad's position was slightly different from that of the other brothers; he was against any terrorist act targeted at France. Whether this was out of caution on his part or these were his true convictions I shall probably never know. Mourad was in favour of *daawa*, the propagation of Islam in France, in other words the indoctrination of the young. This Wahabi explained to me that for 'strategic reasons' we shouldn't open up several fronts at the same time. 'The priority,' he repeated, 'is waging war on the Americans, the Russians and the Jews.'

We arrived at Waterloo station at around half past twelve. The British police were on a war footing after the foiled attack on the London underground and subjected us to a very rigorous check – another racially based check. Our passports were examined by three officers; one of them took them and disappeared into an office, where he stayed for a good fifteen minutes. This wait made Mourad remark that 'Westerners are lacking in intelligence.'

'They still haven't understood,' he told me, 'that the day the brothers come to commit an attack, they won't be wearing beards or *djellabas*.' Finally the British policeman came back with our passports in his hand and said laconically, 'Thank you, sir.'

We hired a car and tried to reach Omar Saiki on the phone. After many attempts, we managed to get him at the other end of the line. We arranged to meet near Edgware Road, in a working-class area of west London which is almost exclusively Muslim. At around 1.30 we got to the street he had suggested. We waited for our brother for a good quarter of an hour before he arrived. He greeted Mourad warmly but gave me the coldest of welcomes. He was aged thirty-three and was wearing jeans, a long winter jacket, and a well-trimmed beard. His height of 1.9m gave him a certain presence. He stayed on the phone and remained distant. He was accompanied by another much older, bearded man with a rucksack who observed our first contact; he was Saiki's bodyguard. I eventually discovered who he was: Rachid Dlimi, one of the former FIS activists who was held in the Folembrey barracks and then placed under house arrest in Burkina Faso. Dlimi had taken refuge in Great Britain a few years before.

After a long phone conversation, Saiki came back and asked, 'Who's Djamel?'

'I am,' I replied.

'Good,' he said with a nod.

Saiki was one of those young upstarts who went through a period of petty crime before finding refuge in Islamism and terrorism, which gave them back their lost self-respect. Saiki doesn't have a great 'service record' in the Islamist movement, but from being a small-time hoodlum without any status when he arrived in France, he ended up being found guilty of heading a terrorist network in 1998. He married a Frenchwoman of Algerian origin who still lives in the suburbs of Paris in Les Muraux. He gained French citizenship, but was stripped of it in September 2002. This undistinguished career makes him act zealously when in the company of his elders who have already proved themselves. I would see this for myself a few minutes later when he changed his tune in the presence of Abdellah Anès, who came to the meeting as arranged, unlike Qamreddine Kherbane, who had pulled out.

We went to a Muslim restaurant. The brothers, who had refused to answer questions on film, were unaware that they were being recorded by my hidden camera, and so they behaved quite naturally. I began with the reason for my visit: I explained to them that I was making a film which would show the injustices which our brothers suffer around the world. Showing total contempt for my colleagues from France 2, Anès asked me to speak only in Arabic.

'It's you I came to see. I don't give a damn about them,' was in essence what he whispered to me.

He had no faith in the French press. I tried to convince him that the majority of the media did their job in an objective manner. At this point Saiki went off at a tangent, and started criticizing France, its judicial system, media, politicians and police force. He was keen to show off in front of Anès. Perhaps he also wanted to show that he was intelligent. I for my part was happy to keep playing the fool.

Saiki ended his 'analysis' of the state of France with veiled threats, turning to my colleagues with a sinister smile: 'There are six million Muslims in France. The majority of them don't support the cause. But you only need three to carry out an attack . . .'

After a two-hour discussion, Abdellah Anès gave me his telephone number and said, 'You are a good brother. Come and see me alone next time. There are a lot of things we can do together. Don't forget that all the brains are here in London.' Anès was evidently trying to recruit me. He said goodbye to me warmly and went off. Having seen Anès's attitude to me, Saiki changed his. 'Monsieur Djamel' became 'my brother Djamel'. I had passed another milestone.

At around 4 p.m., Mourad, Rachid Dlimi, Omar Saiki and I parted company with the France 2 crew to go to the Baker Street mosque for *Maghreb* (sunset) prayers. On the way, Saiki told me that he lived in a room at the Finsbury Park Mosque, run by Abu Hamza. Hamza had even offered him a job; Saiki had been looking after the mosque's bookshop since his arrival in London.

At the Baker Street mosque I ran into dozens of Islamists from all over the world. There were Pakistanis, Egyptians, Yemenis, Saudis, Algerians . . . I even saw two members of the GIA whose names I couldn't remember. One of them acknowledged me, no doubt taking me for someone else. I even saw in the distance an Islamist who came from the same district in Algiers as me. Fortunately from that distance and in my get-up, there was little risk that he would recognize me.

After prayers, we picked up our conversation again. Saiki imitated the attitude of his 'sheikh' Abdellah Anès by asking me to come back alone without 'those other infidels'. I promised him I'd do so in the next few weeks.

We were planning to catch the 9 p.m. train back to Paris. When we left the Baker Street mosque, I asked my brothers to come back with me to meet up with the France 2 crew, who had been waiting for us for over an hour in a café on the Edgware Road. On the way, Saiki spoke at length about jihad and the future of Islamist movements. In his view, what was needed was 'to unify the ranks of the Muslim world to confront the hegemony of the West'. He was convinced that the planet was currently in the throes of a war of religion. He gave a lengthy description of the sorts of action required in France: 'We must,' he repeated, 'explain Islam to all the young people of North African origin and incite them to return to their religion.'

This trip had given me a better understanding of the Islamist network. As Karim had done before him, Mourad had completely faded into the background during our short trip to the British capital. He had scarcely opened his mouth in the presence of Abdellah Anès and Omar Saiki. He only really spoke to me again when we were back on the Eurostar.

At around seven I said goodbye to Saiki and his bodyguard Dlimi, who made a point of giving me the correspondence that he had exchanged with the French ambassador in Burkina Faso, so that I could publicize his case in the media. Saiki repeated his wish to see me 'one to one' as soon as possible. We brought our meeting to an end with the warm embraces which 'brothers' exchange. My trip to London was coming to an end and I was especially satisfied with it as it had gone better than I could have hoped. The brothers hadn't suspected anything. We had been able to film them. We would have some very good footage, which was the most important thing. It would probably be good to go back and see them again before the end of my investigation. But I wasn't at that point yet.

On the train, Mourad and I returned to our discussion of 'Islam and the future of Muslims'. He confessed that his dream was 'to die a martyr in Chechnya or Palestine'. According to what he had told me, he had four children, but even so, he was 'ready to die for the cause' and leave orphans behind. However, what astonished me about what he said was not this, but the fact that he surprised me yet again by claiming that the passport he was travelling with was 'a real fake'.

'Why did you tell me it was genuine?'

'I was afraid you would panic in front of the cops . . .'

'You can't be serious. You're having me on . . .'

'I swear it's false, and they didn't even notice. But be careful, Djamel, don't mention it to the other brothers.'

I had no way of checking whether he had travelled with a false or a genuine passport. I didn't ask him to show it to me, just in case he asked to see mine in return.

THE ARRESTS

From my trip to London, I had confirmation that the British capital had become the sanctuary for hard-core Islamism. Certainly the arrests by Scotland Yard of Abu Qatada, one of Islamism's ideologues, and the recent questioning of some others would not reduce the threat or thwart the extremists' plans.

Writing this book and finalizing my report for France 2 didn't leave me enough time to see the brothers every day. I spoke to Karim on the phone a few times, and he wanted to know 'if the trip had gone well', and I also spoke to Mourad, who said on the phone that he 'just wanted to hear my news'.

That same week I got a message on my answering machine from Ahmed Ouerghemi, the Tunisian Islamist Karim had introduced me to outside the Lariboisière hospital. He wanted to meet me. I called him back and arranged a meeting for the following week.

Although my diary was busy, on Thursday 12 December I managed to get a few minutes during the day to meet Karim.

I wanted to see the lie of the land and find out if there was any news. In the course of our conversation, he gave a strange answer to one of my questions. I don't know why, but that day I got him back on the subject of the brother who had come back from the Caucasus, whom he had spoken about twice during the month of Ramadan. I reiterated my interest in this brother and said I'd like to meet him. Karim promised to talk to him.

'He can't in the next few days. He's preparing for a job . . .'

I understood what 'a job' meant and four days later I discovered who this brother was . . .

Saturday 14 December 2002

Karim had arranged to meet me at 6 p.m. at the restaurant of his friend, Nassreddine, in Belleville. Nassreddine had given an interview on camera for France 2, but now didn't want to be in the film. What he didn't know was that his interview had already been cut because it wasn't interesting enough. He was a former FIS sympathizer who wanted to express his feelings on the political situation in Algeria, which wasn't the angle the film was taking. Although he was already under suspicion by the police for financing terrorism, and had a close relationship with Karim, the restaurateur interested me much less than the other brothers. All the same, I decided to go and see him.

When I arrived, Karim wasn't yet there. I made use of the time to talk to Nassreddine, who shared his fears with me, since he had already had 'problems with the French authorities'. While we were talking, I heard Karim's voice. He wasn't alone; besides Mourad, the Algerian taxi driver, and Sofiane, both of whom I knew, there were five other brothers with him whom I hadn't seen before. Three of them were very young and the other two must have been between thirty and thirty-five.

We sat down at a large table. The brothers wanted to eat. The conversation focused exclusively on religion. Only one of the five newcomers took the time to talk to me; the others remained distant. He introduced himself as Othmane. To try to glean some information about him, I told him that his face looked familiar. He replied curtly that it wasn't possible that we had met before. 'I've only been in France for a month,' he said, to cut short my questions.

But I persisted: 'Where were you before?'

'All over the place. In my village and elsewhere . . .'

Othmane didn't want to tell me more and I for my part decided to restrain my curiosity. Karim suddenly called out to me to ask me not to smoke in his presence. This was the first time he had challenged me like this, though it wasn't the first time that he had seen me smoking a cigarette. He obviously wanted to play the big boss today. I moved table to smoke, and promised him that I would try to finish the cigarette as quickly as possible. The other older man had scarcely said a word to me. All I knew about him was that his first name was Merouane. He must have been about thirty-five and didn't look like an Islamist. In fact, he looked like he could be an 'operational'; in Western clothes he would have gone unnoticed.

Around 7 p.m. we all went to the Omar mosque for the *Icha* (night) prayers. I judged it best not to linger with them, so a quarter of an hour after the end of prayers, I said goodbye and headed off. But that evening something untoward had intrigued me: from the other side of the prayer room, two men aged about thirty had been watching me constantly. At first I thought it was a coincidence, but my suspicions continued to become stronger. In fact, I was being watched. The first man was clean shaven and looked North African; the other man had a fine beard all round his full face. Both were wearing Western clothes. The bearded one was in jeans and a black leather jacket.

When I got outside, I felt calmer – there were no more suspect faces around. I went towards the Couronnes metro station with Mourad's cousin, Mohamed the Tunisian, whom I had bumped into on the way out of the mosque. Before I said goodnight, I asked him to tell Mourad to ring me and then went down into the station. On the platform, I took a newspaper from my rucksack and was about to start reading when I saw the man with the fine beard coming along the platform. He was alone. That was the point at which I started to get worried. When the train came, I made sure I got into a different carriage from the man who was clearly tailing me.

This was the first time I had felt myself being watched like this. Was he a cop? A terrorist? An informer? I never found out. I got off at the Nation station to change train. I couldn't see the man. But my joy was short-lived, as he soon reappeared. By now there could be no doubt: not only was the man following me, but he clearly wanted me to *know* that he was following me.

What followed was an ordeal for me. I left the metro and then, once I was outside, went back in again. The man remained just fifteen metres away from me. He obviously knew that I had noticed him, but that didn't seem to bother him at all. I took another metro train and then got off after two stops and caught a bus. He was still there. But luckily it was busy and I was in a better position than him for getting off. One stop further on, I took advantage of the doors opening near a taxi rank. I quickly jumped into a cab. The man with the beard didn't have time to react. My taxi moved off.

This journey round Paris had lasted more than an hour and

had left me exhausted. As a precaution, I asked the taxi driver to put me down a few hundred metres from my home. I continued my journey on foot in the rain to make sure that I wasn't being followed. I had managed to give the man the slip. But I had the feeling that events were now going to speed up . . .

Monday 16 December 2002

Action stations in the Parisian press. The DST, the direction de surveillance du territoire [anti-terrorist branch], arrested three Islamists in the 'Cité des 4000' housing estate in La Courneuve in the Paris region. The first reports suggested that the three suspected terrorists were preparing an attack in France and were planning to use chemical weapons. Ahmed Belhoud, Mohamed Merbah, and Merouane Benahmed, the three arrested Islamists, had in their possession an NBC suit, a piece of specialist equipment used by those who handle dangerous chemical products.

The name of Merouane Benahmed caught my attention in particular; one of the brothers I had met on the previous Saturday with Karim was also called Merouane. A month before, Karim had told me about this brother who had recently returned from the Caucasus. The information in the press suggested that Merouane Benahmed knew the region. What's more, the man under arrest appeared to have arrived in France in November. There were too many similarities. I was almost sure that Karim and the other brothers were somehow mixed up in it.

Tuesday 17 December 2002

I decided to call Karim and ask to see him. I wanted to get his opinion of these latest arrests and especially find out if he knew the brothers from La Courneuve. I got his answering machine, so I left a message and asked him to call me back. Two hours later my phone rang. It was a colleague telling me that a dispatch from Agence France Presse had just mentioned the arrest of a fourth Islamist. His name was Karim Bourti.

This came as a total surprise. Not the fact of him being arrested, but that the arrest had happened on the day I least expected it. I decided to call Mehdi to get confirmation from him and to find out how the arrest had happened. I knew immediately, though, that Mehdi didn't know anything.

'I'm meeting Karim after the *Asr* prayers,' he told me. I asked him to tell Karim that I was trying to get hold of him. It would have been a blunder if I had told him the news.

At around 6 p.m., Mehdi called me back. 'Brother, brother, Karim has been arrested!' he shouted into the phone. I acted dumb and afraid.

'Really? Why?'

'I don't know. Come to the mosque on the rue Myrrha. I'll see you at seven after the *Icha* prayers.'

'OK. I'll see you soon.'

All the brothers were filled with consternation as a result of the recent arrests that had been made in Islamist circles. From

Belleville to Barbès, no one could talk about anything else. 'We have got to be careful.' That advice had become the watchword. I received several calls from the brothers. Mourad, Sofiane, Mehdi, and Mohamed joined me. They were transfixed. It was as if they were indirectly asking me to stand in for Karim while he was gone. One of them was worried about the money for the prisoners, another was wondering if he should continue with the classes at the mosque, a third hoped that Karim wouldn't tell his interrogators anything. In short, this arrest and those of the previous day had destabilized them. Operationals and their direct support had gone down before an attack could take place and that had shaken them up.

Around 7.30 I met Mehdi on the rue Myrrha. He was in a car driven by Madjid, one of the young brothers I had seen in the restaurant with Karim the Saturday before. I asked Mehdi if we could talk freely in front of this young brother.

'He's sound, Djamel. You've nothing to fear,' he said.

I asked him what reasons he thought could have prompted Karim's arrest. Mehdi didn't know anything. He was worried, but staying objective. 'I've heard that the police are looking for me too.'

'How do you know?'

'They went looking for me in Mantes-la-Jolie.'

'What are you going to do?'

'I think I'll report to the Quai des Orfèvres [police headquarters], but first I want to find out if they have released Karim's wife.'

So his wife had been arrested along with him. Mehdi

suggested that we went to see her together and of course I agreed. In the car I took the opportunity to find out more about it all. My investigation was clearly coming to an end.

'Do you think that Karim knew the brothers from La Courneuve who were arrested yesterday?'

'Of course he knows them. I know them too. We all know each other, Djamel.'

My suspicions were right: Karim was indeed in contact with the 'Chechen ring' and the brothers who were 'operationals'.

Karim's wife was at home with her young brother. She told us what happened when they were arrested. 'There was no fuss,' she added. She told us, too, that they had been questioned in connection with the inquiry the anti-terrorist section was conducting into Richard Reid, the British terrorist who had wanted to blow himself up on a flight from Paris to Miami in December 2001. Mehdi confirmed that he had met Reid and that one of his friends who lived, like him, in Mantes-la-Jolie, had called Karim on his wife's mobile.

After this short conversation, Mehdi went to the headquarters of the anti-terrorist section (the SAT), which is part of the crime squad. I went with him as far as the doors of 36 quai des Orfèvres. It was nearly 11 p.m. That was how I found myself an 'orphan'. The brothers I had had most contact with over the past three months were now in the hands of the police. The report I was filming for France 2 was almost complete. Perhaps this was the end of the adventure . . .

Friday 20 December 2002

After Karim Bourti's arrest my phone didn't stop ringing. The brothers wanted information and I was the one they came to. I absolutely had to go to Belleville for Friday prayers to meet the other members of the group.

At the end of prayers I met Mourad, the Tunisian who had accompanied me to London, his cousin Mohamed, and Ahmed Kheïreddine. Mourad was afraid that the police might have been informed about our visit to the British capital and Ahmed Kheïreddine was expecting to be rearrested. I had to show them that I was in the same boat as them.

'I've received a police summons. I've got to go next Monday.'

This was yet another ploy and would enable me to disappear without arousing the brothers' suspicions before my report appeared on television and this book came out. I saw anxiety appear on my brothers' faces. Mourad was especially concerned. At that very moment, my phone rang. It was Mehdi. He'd been released.

'They've released Karim and me. But you must be careful. The police were asking about you. Karim wants to see you on Monday.'

This news of their release came as a surprise. When they heard it, the brothers all said, '*Alhamdou lillah* [God be praised],' in unison. I chose that precise moment to leave them; I was afraid that the police might have inadvertently revealed my true identity to Karim or Mehdi. Since the start of my investigation, no one except a handful of people close to me had known that I was in touch with the Islamists. My fears grew when Mehdi asked me to come and see them in the rue Myrrha without telling the other brothers.

'Tell Karim that I can't come today. I've got some problems to sort out.'

I wanted to be sure that the brothers still knew nothing about me. I decided to let things take their course, to test Karim's reaction before going to see him the following Monday. No information about Karim's release had filtered through. I left my phone switched off all weekend to give me time to think.

Monday 23 December 2002

When I listened to my answering machine, I found the brothers had left twelve messages. Karim had rung four times. From the tone of his voice, I reckoned that he didn't know anything about me. He even thanked me for showing concern about how he was. My intuition told me that I could continue for a few more days.

I went to hang around in the Belleville district and waited for him to try to call me again. That way, I wouldn't give him time to react when he rang, as I would be just a few minutes from his home. I wasn't wrong. At twelve on the dot, Karim phoned. He asked me to meet him at his apartment.

'I'm in your neighbourhood just now.'

'Come up to the house, Djamel, I'm alone.'

Karim was still feeling distressed by his four days in custody. Pale but still smiling, he greeted me very enthusiastically, and I for my part showed my satisfaction at seeing him free again. He told me the details of his interrogation.

'I thought I was going to get two years . . .'

'Why did they arrest you?'

'Because of the Richard Reid case.'

'Did they know that you knew the people from La Courneuve?'

'No, thank God.'

I had caught him out. Karim had never told me that he

knew the members of the group arrested at La Courneuve, who had been taken in the day before his own arrest. We hadn't had time to talk about it. It was Mehdi who had confided that they knew each other. Karim now replied to my questions without any distrust. In fact he said that his trust in me was 'total'.

'It's at difficult times that you know who the true brothers are. And now we know, Djamel, that we can count on you. Mehdi and my wife said that you were really worried about us.'

'That's natural, Karim. Believers are brothers.'

'Yes, we're brothers. We're brothers in religion but we're also brothers in arms.'

'What do you mean by that?'

'They're arresting us one after another. Well, if they want bombs to go off, we'll give them bombs with God's help. And to do that, we have to count on all the brothers. Everyone must know that we are at war – it's jihad, Djamel. Jihad is an obligation for everyone. You must be ready.'

Karim was now speaking to me directly. He counted me as one of their own. I went on to ask him about how the police had talked about me when he was being questioned.

'My phone was tapped. They just asked who you were.'

'What did you tell them?'

'I didn't tell them anything. I presented you as a brother who's a journalist, that's all.'

Karim asked me to be very vigilant and not to talk too much on the phone any more. He was aware that he was now under close surveillance. I left him, having agreed that we would meet at the end of the week.

Friday 27 December 2002

I went to Friday prayers, as usual, in Belleville. All the brothers were there. During the week there had been other arrests in Islamist circles, in particular of those who were close to the Chechen network. The militants who were picked up were planning to commit attacks against Russian targets in France. The brothers spoke of nothing but this. They remained worried, as they were convinced that the arrests were going to continue.

I saw Karim after the prayers. He was with a group of young brothers to whom he was giving religious instruction. Each one of them was a potential Djamel Loiseau. They talked about religion but also about jihad. One of them, Madjid, the one who was with Mehdi on the day of Karim's arrest, worried me especially. He had the profile of those second-generation North Africans who have been brought back to Islam and who are ready to follow their guru's teaching to the letter. Madjid was of interest to Karim on several counts: he was young, of North African origin – and he worked at Charles de Gaulle airport.

I made small talk with Karim before heading off. He was especially keen to know the date when the film I had made for France 2 would be broadcast. I told him it was scheduled for the end of January and promised to keep him posted. After our brief conversation, we agreed to meet again the following week.

Tuesday 31 December 2002

Appointment with Ahmed Ouerghemi, the Tunisian Islamist who has no hesitation in sending the Tunisian president death threats by fax and post. I had arranged to meet him to interview him for the new report I was planning to make for the M6 channel. He was of interest to me as he dealt in forged documents. I wanted to catch him red-handed with my hidden camera. During our interview he held forth in the usual way against the Tunisian regime, George Bush and Ariel Sharon, and in support of worldwide Islamist movements. He was the last Islamist I would meet during 2002.

Now I had no problem moving around in Islamist circles. I had become one of them and they refused me nothing. I had maintained that I would pursue this last investigation with them until mid-January before disappearing and returning to my life, my family and my friends.

EPILOGUE

My time undercover was coming to an end. I had decided to maintain contact until 20 January 2003, at the latest, the day before this book was published. I had also agreed to continue my investigation for the *Forbidden Zone* programme on M6, which was being made through a production company.

I was determined to withdraw discreetly before the people who had thought of me as their brother for over three months discovered my true identity.

Karim, Mehdi, Mourad, Sofiane, Mohamed, Ahmed, Omar, Abdellah, Redha and all the others are Islamists. That means they are potential terrorists. I talked, ate, prayed and laughed with them. At no time was I susceptible to their words or to their theories. The whole experience was very instructive for me: from a professional point of view it had allowed me to confirm my ideas about Islamism. Whether it is driven by a Wahabi ideology or by that of the brotherhood of the 'Muslim brothers', Islamic fundamentalism remains a scourge that needs to be eradicated, a form of fascism which must be fought. I noticed throughout my whole time with them, the significance which the people I called my brothers accorded to double-speak, which explains the importance to them of appearances, and which they use to hide what they really are and what they really think: what they call *takiya*. From a personal point of view, this experience allowed me to live with people I have always fought against and encounter the depravity of a mentality which refuses all difference, all dialogue, and preaches above all the negation of others.

My friends and colleagues have asked me a question: did I at any time feel sympathy towards these brothers whom I had in reality betrayed? Did I feel any remorse? Any qualms? My answer is emphatically no.

It is no because their behaviour, their apparent kindness, and their good manners were all intended for Djamel Mostaghanemi, their 'brother', not Mohamed Sifaoui. If they had got wind of Sifaoui's beliefs, they would certainly have killed him as they have killed or would like to kill all those who do not pay allegiance to Islamism. I saw their false smiles for my colleagues from France 2 before they called them 'filthy infidels'. I heard their language of hate. I saw their contempt for life. I heard their hymn to death.

And because I was aware of this, I was mentally fore-armed against any possibility of 'Stockholm syndrome'. My 'brothers', I shall never forget, are first and foremost murderous brothers.

EPILOGUE TO THE ENGLISH EDITION

On 22 January 2003, the eve of the publication of this book in France, Karim Bourti and Mehdi Terranova were arrested by the anti-terrorist branch of the police. A charge of GBH had been brought against them by a representative of an Islamic Association who had been attacked by a group of Islamists on 21 December 2002 as he was leaving the Jean-Pierre Timbaud mosque. He had identified my two 'brothers' among his attackers. The anti-terrorist magistrates decided to interview Karim and Mehdi under caution. Karim and Mehdi were subsequently locked up in the Santé prison in Paris.

I hadn't known about this attack, which took place the day following Karim Bourti's release in December, after the police had interviewed him in connection with the Richard Reid case. When I met him again on 23 December, he made no mention of the attack. I only realized afterwards that, in hiding the incident from me, Karim had shown that he didn't fully trust me.

However, between finishing this book and Karim's arrest on

22 January, several things had happened: first of all, I spent a few days filming in order to finalize the report I was making for the M6 channel.

In mid-January I decided to accompany Karim and some others to London. He wanted to meet Omar Saiki and deliver a sum of money to him. This gave me the opportunity to meet the former head of the GSPC in France again. I retain two memories of this trip in particular: the interrogation to which I was subjected by the British police when I got off the Eurostar (whereas Karim passed through without a hitch), and the discussion I had with Omar Saiki about 'traitors'.

The first memory provided anecdotal confirmation of something I already believed: that the British police still have a lot to learn about the fight against terrorism. What other explanation could there be for the fact that on my previous trip with Mourad on 8 December 2002, he had managed to cross the border with a false passport (a fact which I have had time to verify) without the British or French police noticing? And how else can one explain that during my journey with Karim, I – the false Islamist who had never been condemned – was subject to a check, while Karim – the true Islamist who had been imprisoned for a terrorist offence – was able to breeze through without anyone paying any attention to him?

The second memory which I won't forget in a hurry took place in an Edgware Road restaurant where we had gone to have a meal with Omar Saiki. I had begun to get on well with him. We were talking about politics, France, the future of the 'armed struggle' amongst other things, when he brought up the subject of the fate which is reserved for 'traitors'. He didn't mince his words.

'Those who betray us should have their throats cut. Them and their families,' he said with a ferocious smile, looking me in the eye and checking my reaction.

Continuing to meet his gaze, I replied: 'You're right, my brother. They should have their throats cut.'

Seeing that I hadn't reacted badly, he went on to talk about other things.

There was an explanation for Omar Saiki's thinly veiled threats. During our short stay in London, Karim Bourti told me that he was going to talk to Saiki in order to have him entrust me with important missions. In the context of the reorganization of the network he wanted me to play a coordinating role between the different cells of the GSPC in Europe. 'You can travel without any problem since you are a journalist,' he said when he asked if I agreed to take part in the jihad.

I could have accepted the role in order to take my investigation further, but I decided at that precise moment to stop my under-cover operation; I had reached the limits of journalism, and to have gone further would have caught me in my own trap and landed me in situations which were unmanageable both ethically and legally. And so on my return to Paris I decided to call a halt to my investigation.

A few days after the publication of my book in France, I started to receive threatening phone calls and I lodged a complaint. Karim Bourti's wife was one of the people who threatened me. The matter is now in the hands of the police.

By contrast, I was sincerely moved by the signs of sympathy and the numerous letters which I received from readers in France, especially from Muslims. A Muslim woman ended her letter thus: 'Thank you for showing that not all Muslims are potential terrorists.' Many people wondered why I took 'so many risks'. They will find part of my answer in the letter I have just quoted.